Collins

KU-756-994

SCOTLAND

Contents

Published by Collins
An imprint of HarperCollins Publishers
77-85 Fulham Palace Road, Hammersmith, London W6 8JB

www.harpercollins.co.uk

Copyright © HarperCollins Publishers Ltd 2009
Collins® is a registered trademark of HarperCollins Publishers Limited
Mapping generated from Collins Bartholomew digital databases

Mapping on pages 29-59 uses map data licensed from Ordnance Survey ®
with the permission of the Controller of Her Majesty's Stationery Office.
© Crown copyright. Licence number 399302

The grid on this map is the National Grid taken from the Ordnance Survey map with the
permission of the Controller of Her Majesty's Stationery Office.

Key to road map pages

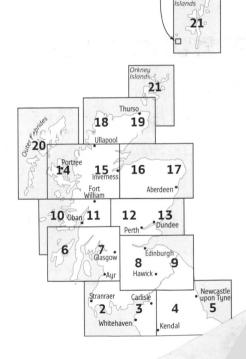

The representation of a roa...
right of way.

Printed in Hong Kong   ISBN

WC12407 / UDA   mail: r...

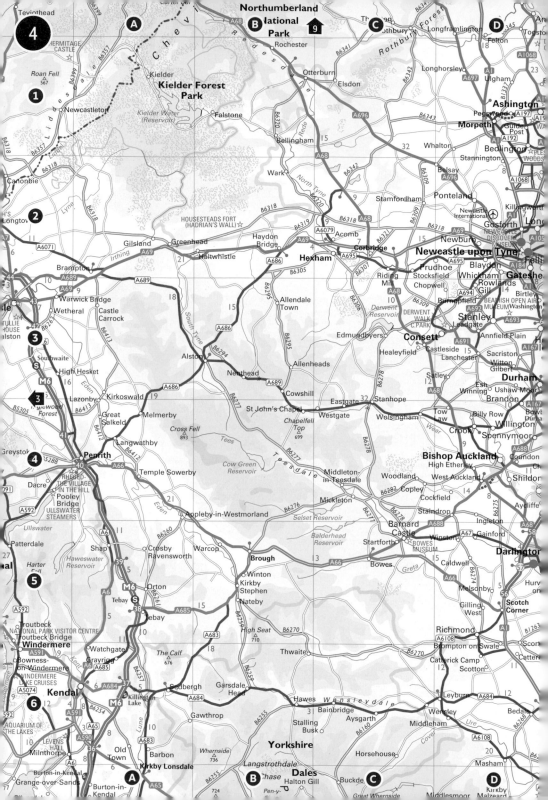

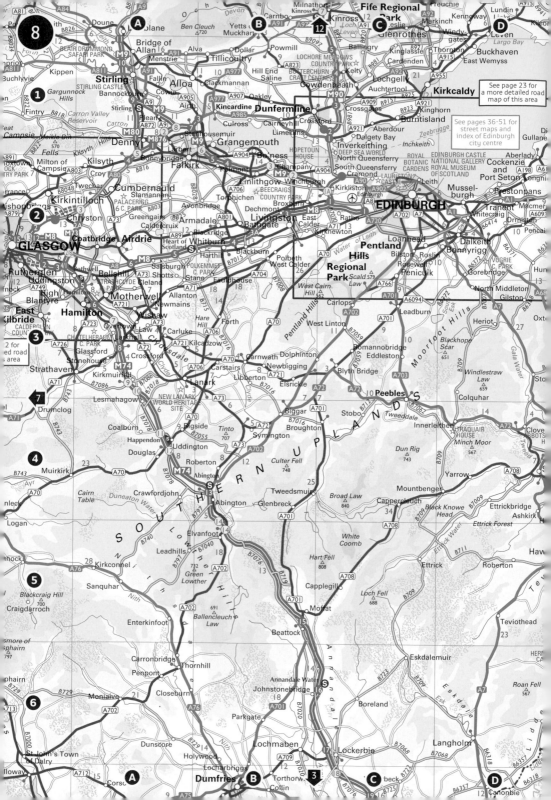

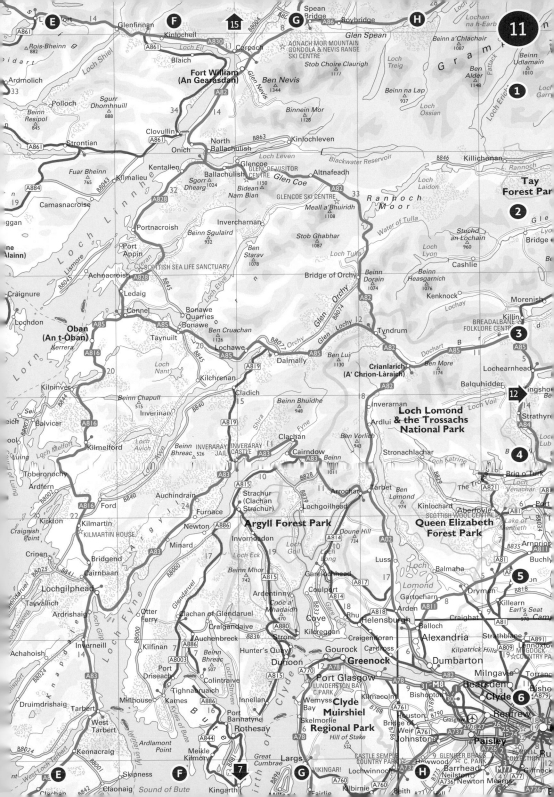

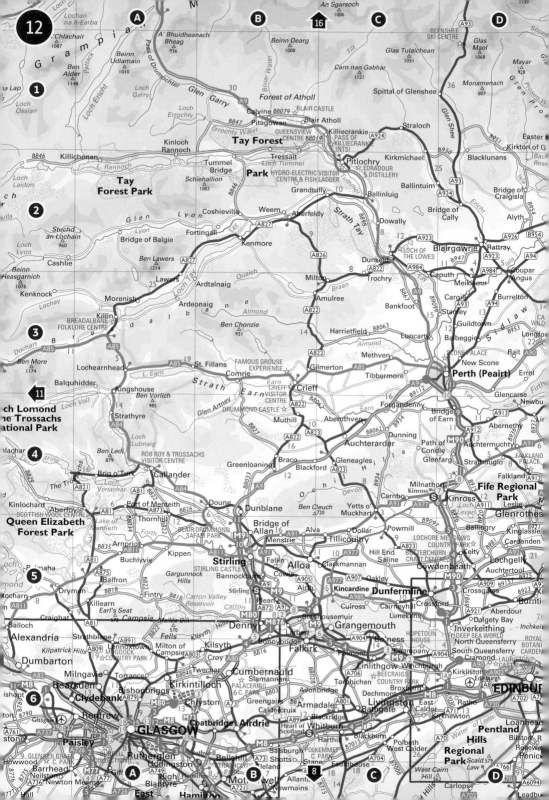

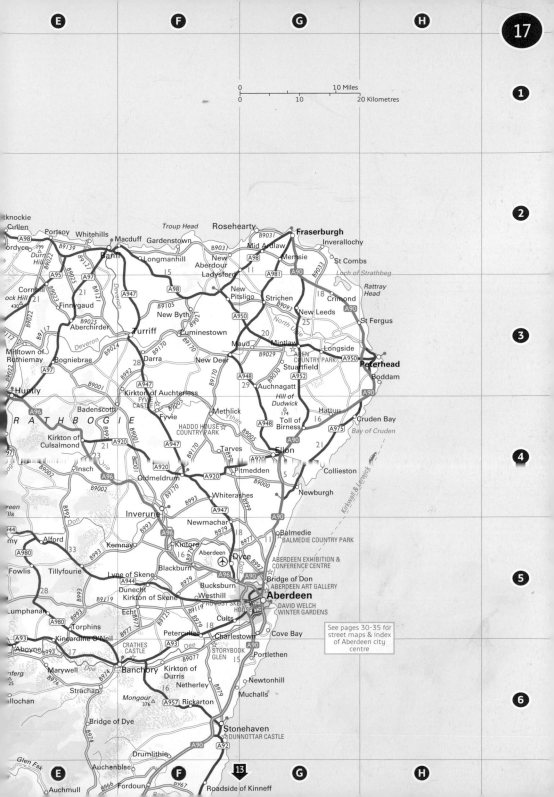

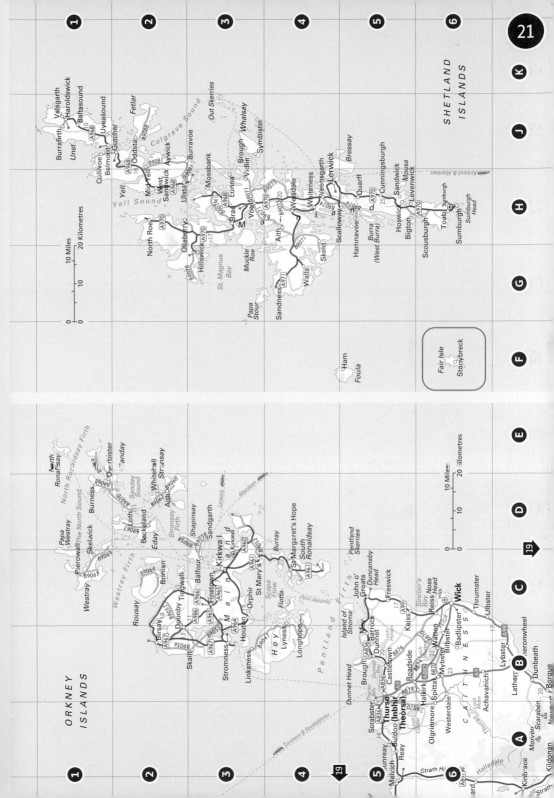

SHETLAND ISLANDS

ORKNEY ISLANDS

Fair Isle
Stonybreck

Out Skerries

Colgrave Sound

Yell Sound

Valsgarth
Haroldswick
Burrafirth
Uyeasound
Baltasound
Unst
Belmont
A968
Fetlar
Cullivoe
Gutcher
Oddsta
Mid Yell
West Sandwick
Yell
Ulsta
Burravoe
Mossbank
Whalsay
Symbister
Brough
Vidlin
Lunna
Brae
Voe
Aith
Whiteness
Weisdale
Lerwick
Veensgarth
Bressay
Scalloway
Quarff
Cunningsburgh
Sandwick
Mousa
Levenwick
Hoswick
Bigton
Scousburgh
Sumburgh
Sumburgh Head
Toab

North Roe
Ollaberry
Hillswick
Burra (West Burra)
Hamnavoe
Skeld
Walls
Sandness
Muckle Roe
Papa Stour
St. Magnus Bay

Ham
Foula

North Ronaldsay
North Ronaldsay Firth
Papa Westray
Westray
Rousay
Pierowall
Skelwick
Burness
Loth
Eday
Sanday
Sanday Sound
Whiteh'll
Stronsay
Shapinsay
Backeland
Brinian
Tingwall
Doonby
Finstown
Birsay
Skaill
Stromness
Linksness
Hoy
Lyness
Longhope
Mainland
Kirkwall
Balfour
Orphir
Houton
St Mary's
Burray
South Ronaldsay
St Margaret's Hope
Scapa Flow
Flotta
Pentland Skerries
Westray Firth
The North Sound
Stronsay Firth
Pentland Firth
Island of Stroma

Dunnet Head
Brough
Barrock
Castletown
Dunnet
Duncansby Head
John o' Groats
Freswick
Sinclair's Bay
Reiss
Noss Head
Wick
Thrumster
Ulbster
Lybster
Scrabster
Thurso (Inbhir Theorsa)
Reay
Halkirk
Westerdale
Bilbster
Watten
Spittal
Mybster
Badlipster
Kaiss
Roadside
Brough
Latheron
Dunbeath
Borgue
Newport
CAITHNESS

ORKNEY ISLANDS

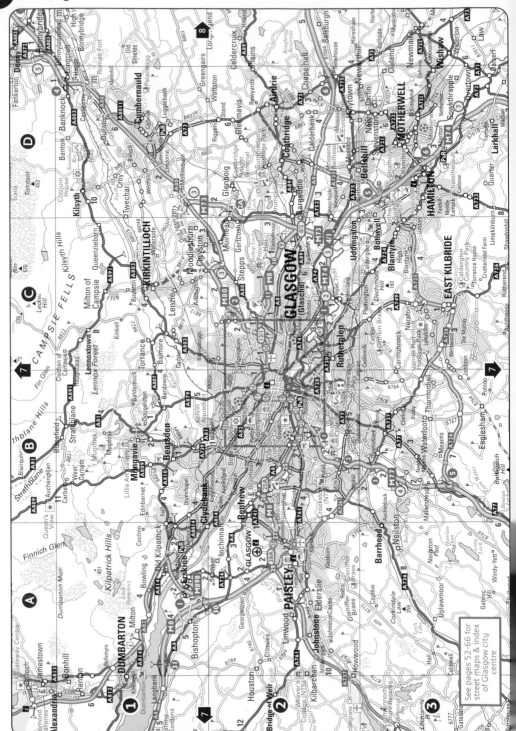

See pages 52-66 for street maps & index of Glasgow city centre

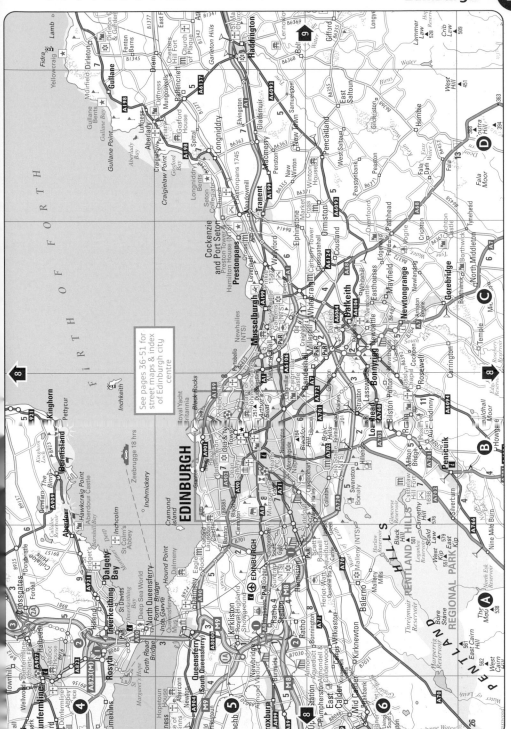

0   1   2   3   4   5 miles

0 1 2 3 4 5 6 7 8 km

See pages 36–51 for street maps & index of Edinburgh city centre

Administrative area abbreviations

Aber.	Aberdeenshire	E.Renf.	East Renfrewshire	Northumb.	Northumberland	Shet.	Shetland
Arg. & B.	Argyll & Bute	Edin.	Edinburgh	Ork.	Orkney	Stir.	Stirling
Cumb.	Cumbria	High.	Highland	P. & K.	Perthshire & Kinross	T. & W.	Tyne & Wear
D. & G.	Dumfries & Galloway	I.o.M.	Isle of Man	Renf.	Renfrewshire	W.Dun.	West Dunbartonshire
Dur.	Durham	Midloth.	Midlothian	S.Ayr.	South Ayrshire	W. Isles	Western Isles
E.Ayr.	East Ayrshire	N.Lan.	North Lanarkshire	S.Lan.	South Lanarkshire		(Na h-Eileanan an Iar)
E.Loth.	East Lothian	N.Yorks.	North Yorkshire	Sc.Bord.	Scottish Borders	W. Loth.	West Lothian

Index entries shown in **bold** type can be found on the urban area maps, pages 22-23

A

Abbeytown 3 G3
Aberchirder 17 E3
Aberdeen 17 G5
Aberdeen Airport 17 F5
Aberdour 8 C1
Aberdour 23 A4
Aberfeldy 12 B2
Aberfoyle 7 H1
Aberlady 8 D1
Aberlady 23 D4
Aberlemno 13 F2
Aberlour 16 C3
Abernethy 12 D4
Aberuthven 12 C4
Abhainnsuidhe 20 C4
Abington 8 B4
Aboyne 17 E6
Abronhill 22 D1
Achadh Mòr 20 E3
Achahoish 6 D3
Acharacle 10 D1
Achavanich 19 G3
Achfary 18 B3
Achiltibuie 18 A5
Achintee 15 E3
Achnacroish 11 E2
Achnasheen 15 F3
Achosnich 10 C1
Achriesgill 18 B3
Acomb 4 C2
Aird Asaig 20 D4
Aird of Sleat 14 C5
Airdrie 8 A2
Airdrie 22 D2
Airidh a'Bhruaich 20 D4
Airth 8 A1
Aith Ork. 21 D2
Aith Shet. 21 H4
Akeld 9 G4
Alexandria 7 G3
Alford 17 E5
Allanton N.Lan. 8 A3
Allanton S.Lan. 22 D3
Allendale Town 4 B3
Allenheads 4 B3
Allnabad 18 C3
Alloa 8 A1
Allonby 3 F3
Alloway 7 G6
Alness 15 H2
Alnmouth 9 H5
Alnwick 9 H5
Alston 4 B3
Altnafeadh 11 G2
Altnaharra 18 D4
Alva 8 A1
Alves 16 C2
Alvie 16 A5
Alyth 12 D2
Amble 9 H5
Ambleside 3 H5
Amulree 12 B3
Ancroft 9 G3
Ancrum 9 E4
Andreas 2 C5
Annan 3 G2
Annfield Plain 4 D3
Anniesland 22 B2
Anstruther 13 F4
Aoradh 6 A3
Appleby-in-
   Westmorland 4 A4
Applecross 14 D3
Arbirlot 13 F2
Arbroath 13 F2
Ardchiavaig 6 B1

Arden 7 G2
Ardentinny 7 F2
Ardeonaig 12 A3
Ardersier 16 A3
Ardfern 6 D1
Ardgay 15 H1
Ardlui 7 G1
Ardlussa 6 C2
Ardmair 15 F1
Ardminish 6 B3
Ardmolich 11 E1
Ardrishaig 6 D2
Ardrossan 7 F4
Ardtalnaig 12 A3
Ardtoe 10 D1
Ardvasar 14 C5
Arinagour 10 B2
Arisaig 14 C6
Armadale 8 B2
Arnisdale 14 D5
Arniston Engine 23 C6
Arnol 20 E2
Arnprior 7 H2
Arrochar 7 G1
Ashgill 22 D3
Ashington 4 D1
Ashkirk 8 D4
Aspatria 3 G3
Attadale 15 E4
Auchallater 16 C6
Auchenback 22 B3
Auchenblae 13 G1
Auchenbreck 7 E2
Auchencairn 3 E3
Auchencrow 9 F2
Auchendinny 23 B6
Auchindrain 7 E1
Auchinleck 7 H5
Auchinloch 22 C1
Auchmull 13 F1
Auchnagatt 17 G3
Auchterarder 12 C4
Auchtermuchty 12 D4
Auchtertool 8 C1
Auldearn 16 B3
Auldhouse 22 C3
Aultbea 14 D1
Aultguish Inn 15 G2
Aviemore 16 A5
Avoch 15 H3
Avonbridge 8 B2
Aycliffe 4 D4
Aysgarth 4 C6
Aywick 21 J2

B

Backaland 21 D2
Badcaul 15 E1
Badenscoth 17 E4
Badintagairt 18 C5
Badlipster 19 G3
Baile Mhartainn 20 B6
Baile Mòr 10 B3
Baillieston 22 C2
Bainbridge 4 C6
Balallan 20 D3
Balbeggie 12 D3
Balblair 15 G2
Baldernock 22 B1
Balemartine 10 A2
Balephuil 10 A2
Balerno 23 A6
Balfour 21 D3
Balfron 7 H2
Balgown 14 B2
Balintore 16 A2
Balivanich 20 B7

Ballabeg 2 B6
Ballachulish 11 F2
Ballantrae 2 A1
Ballasalla 2 B6
Ballater 16 D6
Ballaugh 2 C5
Ballencrieff 23 D5
Ballingry 8 C1
Ballinluig 12 C2
Ballintuim 12 D2
Balloch N.Lan. 22 D1
Balloch W.Dun. 7 G2
Ballochan 17 E6
Ballochroy 6 D4
Ballygrant 6 B3
Balmacara 14 D4
Balmaha 7 G2
Balmedie 17 G5
Balmore 22 C1
Balnacra 15 E3
Balnahard 10 C3
Balnapaling 16 A2
Balquhidder 12 A3
Baltasound 21 J1
Balvicar 6 D1
Bamburgh 9 H4
Banchory 17 F6
Banff 17 E2
Bankfoot 12 C3
Banknock 22 D1
Bannockburn 8 A1
Banton 22 D1
Barassie 7 G5
Barbaraville 16 A2
Barbon 4 A6
Bardowie 22 B1
Bargeddie 22 C2
Bargrennan 2 C2
Barnard Castle 4 C5
Barnton 23 A5
Barr 2 B1
Barra (Tràigh Mhòr)
   Airport 20 A9
Barrapoll 10 A2
Barrhead 7 H4
Barrhead 22 A3
Barrhill 2 B1
Barrock 19 G2
Barvas 20 E2
Bathgate 8 B2
Beadnell 9 H4
Bearsden 7 H3
Bearsden 22 B1
Beattock 8 B5
Beauly 15 H3
Bedale 4 D6
Bedlington 4 D1
Beith 7 G4
Belford 9 H4
Bellingham 4 B1
Bellshill 8 A3
Bellshill 22 D2
Bellsmyre 22 A1
Belmont 21 J1
Belsay 4 D2
Benbecula (Balivanich)
   Airport 20 B7
Bernisdale 14 B3
Berriedale 19 G4
Berwick-upon-Tweed 9 G3
Bettyhill 19 E2
Biggar 8 B4
Bigton 21 H5
Bilbster 19 G3
Billingham 5 E4
Billy Row 4 D4
Bilston 8 C2
Bilston 23 B6
Birdston 22 C1

Birsay 21 B2
Birtley 4 D3
Bishop Auckland 4 D4
Bishopbriggs 7 H3
Bishopbriggs 22 C1
Bishopton 7 G3
Bishopton 22 A1
Blackburn Aber. 17 F5
Blackburn W.Loth. 8 B2
Blackford 12 B4
Blackhall Edin. 23 B5
Blackhall Renf. 22 A2
Blackhall Colliery 5 E4
Blacklunans 12 D1
Blackridge 8 A2
Blackwaterfoot 7 E5
Blaich 11 F1
Blair Atholl 12 B1
Blairgowrie 12 D2
Blaydon 4 D2
Blyth 5 E1
Blyth Bridge 8 C3
Boat of Garten 16 B5
Boath 15 H2
Boddam 17 H3
Bogniebrae 17 E3
Boldon 5 E2
Boltby 5 E6
Bolton 9 E2
Bonar Bridge 15 H1
Bonawe 11 F3
Bonawe Quarries 11 F3
Bonchester Bridge 9 E5
Bo'ness 8 B1
Bonjedward 9 E4
Bonnington 23 A6
Bonnybridge 8 A1
Bonnyrigg 8 D2
Bonnyrigg 23 C6
Bootle 3 G6
Boreland 3 G1
Boreraig 14 A3
Borgh 20 D2
Borgue D. & G. 2 D3
Borgue High. 19 G4
Borrowdale 3 H5
Borve High. 14 B3
Borve W.Isles 20 E2
Bothel 3 G4
Bothwell 22 D3
Bournmoor 5 E2
Bowburn 5 E4
Bowes 4 C5
Bowling 22 A1
Bowmore 6 B4
Bowness-on-Solway 3 G2
Bowness-on-
   Windermere 3 H6
Braaid 2 C6
Bracadale 14 B4
Braco 12 B4
Bracora 14 D6
Brae 21 H3
Braeantra 15 H2
Braehead 22 B2
Braemar 16 C6
Bragar 20 D2
Braithwaite 3 G4
Brampton 4 A2
Brandon 4 D4
Breakish 14 C4
Breanais 20 C3
Breascleit 20 D3
Brechin 13 F1
Bridge of Allan 8 A1
Bridge of Balgie 12 A2
Bridge of Cally 12 D2

Bridge of Craigisla 12 D2
Bridge of Don 17 G5
Bridge of Dun 13 F2
Bridge of Dye 17 E6
Bridge of Earn 12 D4
Bridge of Orchy 11 H3
Bridge of Weir 7 G3
Bridgend Angus 13 F1
Bridgend (Islay)
   Arg. & B. 6 B3
Bridgend (Lochgilphead)
   Arg. & B. 6 D2
Bridgend Moray 16 D4
Bridgeton 22 C2
Brig o'Turk 7 H1
Brigham 3 F4
Brinian 21 C2
Broadford 14 C4
Brochel 14 C3
Brodick 7 E5
Brompton 5 E6
Brompton on Swale 4 D5
Brora 19 H1
Brotton 5 F4
Brough Cumb. 4 B5
Brough High. 19 G2
Brough Shet. 21 J3
Broughton 8 C4
Broughton in
   Furness 3 G6
Broughty Ferry 13 E3
Broxburn 8 B2
Buchlyvie 7 H2
Buckhaven 8 D1
Buckie 16 D2
Bucksburn 17 F5
Buldoo 19 F2
Bunessan 10 C3
Burgh by Sands 3 H3
Burghead 16 C2
Burness 21 D1
Burnhouse 7 G4
Burniston 5 H6
Burnmouth 9 G2
Burnopfield 4 D3
Burntisland 8 C1
Burntisland 23 B4
Burrafirth 21 J1
Burravoe 21 J2
Burrelton 12 D3
Busby 22 B3
Buttermere 3 G5

C

Cadder 22 C1
Cadzow 22 D3
Cairnbaan 6 D2
Cairndow 7 F1
Cairneyhill 8 B1
Cairnryan 2 A2
Caldbeck 3 H4
Calderbank 22 D2
Caldercruix 8 A2
Calderglen 22 C3
Caldwell E.Renf. 22 A3
Caldwell N.Yorks. 4 D5
Calgary 10 B2
Callander 7 H1
Calvine 12 B1
Camasnacroise 11 E2
Cambuslang 22 C2
Campbeltown (Ceann Loch
   Chille Chiarain) 6 D6
Campbeltown Airport 6 C5
Camps 23 A6
Camptown 9 E5
Cannich 15 G4
Canonbie 3 H2
Caolas 10 A2

Caplaw 22 A3
Cappercleuch 8 C4
Capplegill 8 C5
Caputh 12 C2
Carbeth 22 B1
Carbost (Loch Snizort Beag)
　High. 14 B3
Carbost (Loch Harport)
　High. 14 B4
Carbrain 22 D1
Cardenden 8 C1
Cardonald 22 B2
Cardross 7 G3
Carfin 22 D3
Cargenbridge 3 F2
Cargill 12 D3
Carlisle 3 H3
Carlops 8 C3
Carloway 20 D2
Carluke 8 A3
Carmunnock 22 B3
Carmyle 22 C2
Carmyllie 13 F2
Carnbee 13 F4
Carnbo 12 C4
Carnoustie 13 F3
Carntyne 22 C2
Carnwath 8 B3
Carradale 6 D5
Carrbridge 16 B4
Carrington 23 C6
Carronbridge 3 E1
Carsaig 10 D3
Carsluith 2 C3
Carsphairn 2 D1
Carstairs 8 B3
Cashlie 11 H2
Castle Carrock 4 A3
Castle Douglas 3 E2
Castle Kennedy 2 B3
Castlebay (Bàgh a'
　Chaisteil) 20 A10
Castlecary 22 D1
Castlemilk 22 C3
Castleside 4 C3
Castleton 5 F5
Castletown *High.* 19 G2
Castletown *I.o.M.* 2 B6
Cathcart 22 B2
Cathkin 22 C3
Catrine 7 H5
Catterick 4 D6
Catterick Camp 4 D6
Cawdor 16 A3
Cayton 5 H6
Ceann a' Bhàigh 20 B6
Cearsiadar 20 E3
Ceres 13 E4
Champany 8 B2
Chapelhall 22 D2
Charlestown 17 G5
Chatton 9 G4
Chester-le-Street 4 D3
Chesters 9 E5
Chilton 4 D4
Chirnside 9 F3
Chopwell 4 D3
Christon Bank 9 H4
Chryston 7 H3
Chryston 22 C1
Cille Bhrighde 20 B9
Clabhach 10 B2
Clachan (Loch Fyne)
　Arg. & B. 7 F1
Clachan (Kintyre)
　Arg. & B. 6 D4
Clachan *High.* 14 C4
**Clachan of
　Campsie 22 C1**
Clachan of
　Glendaruel 7 E2
Clachtoll 18 A4
Clackmannan 8 B1
Cladich 11 F3
Claggan 11 E2
Claonaig 6 D4
Clarkston 22 B3
Clashmore 16 A1
Clashnessie 18 A4

Cleadale 14 B6
Cleadon 5 E2
Cleator Moor 3 F5
Cleland 4 A3
Cleland 22 D3
Clermiston 23 A5
Closeburn 3 E1
Cloughton 5 H6
Clova 13 E1
Clovenfords 8 D4
Clovullin 11 F5
Clunes 15 F6
Clydebank 7 H3
Clydebank 22 A1
Coalburn 8 A4
Coast 15 E1
Coatbridge 8 A2
Coatbridge 22 D2
Cochno 22 A1
Cock Bridge 16 C5
Cockburnspath 9 F2
Cockenzie & Port
　Seton 8 D2
**Cockenzie and Port
　Seton 23 D5**
Cockermouth 3 G4
Cockfield 4 D4
Cockpen 23 C6
Coldingham 9 F2
Coldstream 9 F4
Colinton 23 B6
Colintraive 7 E3
Collieston 17 G4
Collin 3 F2
Colmonell 2 B1
Colnabaichin 16 C5
Colquhar 8 D3
Comrie 12 B3
Condorrat 22 D1
Coniston 3 H6
Connel 11 F3
Conon Bridge 15 H3
Consett 4 D3
Contin 15 G3
Copley 4 C4
Corbridge 4 C2
Cornhill 17 E3
Cornhill-on-Tweed 9 F4
Corpach 11 G1
Corrie 7 E4
Corsock 3 E2
Corstorphine 23 A5
Coshieville 12 B2
Coulport 7 F2
Coundon 4 D4
Coupar Angus 12 D2
Cousland 23 C6
Cove *Arg. & B.* 7 F2
Cove *High.* 14 D1
Cove Bay 17 G5
Cowdenbeath 8 C1
Cowie 8 A1
Cowshill 4 B3
Coylton 7 G6
Coylumbridge 16 B5
Craichie 13 E2
Craig 15 E3
Craigandaive 7 E2
Craigdarroch 7 H6
Craigellachie 16 C3
Craigendoran 7 G2
Craighat 7 G2
Craigielaw 23 D5
Craiglockhart 23 B5
Craigmillar 23 B5
Craigneuk 22 D3
Craignure 11 E3
Crail 13 F4
Cramlington 4 D2
Cramond 8 C2
Cramond 23 A5
Cranshaws 9 E2
Crask Inn 18 D4
Craster 9 H4
Crathie 16 C6
Crawfordjohn 8 A4
Creagorry 20 B7
Creetown 2 C3
Cregneash 2 B6

Crianlarich (A' Chrìon-
　Làraich) 11 H3
Crichton 23 C6
Crieff 12 B3
Crimond 17 G3
Crinan 6 D2
Crocketford (Ninemile
　Bar) 3 E2
Croick 15 G1
Cromarty 16 A2
Crook 4 D4
Crookham 9 G4
Crosbost 20 E3
Crosby Ravensworth 4 A5
Crossaig 6 D4
Crosscanonby 3 F4
Crossford *Fife* 8 B1
Crossford *S.Lan.* 8 A3
Crossgatehall 23 C6
Crossgates 8 C1
Crossgates 23 A4
Crosshands 7 G5
Crosshill 7 G6
Crosshouse 7 G5
Crosslee 22 A2
Crossmichael 3 E2
Croy *High.* 16 A3
Croy *N.Lan.* 8 A2
Croy *N.Lan.* 22 D1
Cruden Bay 17 G4
Crutherland Farm 22 C3
Culbokie 15 H3
Culdrain 17 E4
Cullen 17 E2
Cullicudden 15 H2
Cullipool 6 D1
Cullivoe 21 J1
Culnacraig 18 A5
Culnaknock 14 C2
Culross 8 B1
Cults 17 F5
Cumbernauld 8 A2
Cumbernauld 22 D1
Cuminestown 17 F3
Cumnock 7 H5
Cunningsburgh 21 H5
Cupar 13 E4
Currie 23 A6

D
Dacre 3 H4
Dailly 7 F6
Dairsie 13 E4
Dalabrog 20 B8
Dalbeattie 3 E2
Dalby 2 B6
Dalgety Bay 8 C1
Dalgety Bay 23 A4
Dalkeith 8 D2
Dalkeith 23 C6
Dallas 16 C3
Dalmally 11 G3
Dalmellington 7 G6
Dalmeny 23 A5
Dalmuir 22 A1
Dalnavie 15 H2
Dalry 7 F4
Dalrymple 7 G6
Dalserf 22 D3
Dalston 3 H3
Dalwhinnie 15 H6
Danby 5 G5
Danderhall 23 C6
Darlington 4 D5
Darra 17 F3
Darvel 7 H5
Dava 16 B4
Daviot 16 A4
Dearham 3 F4
Dechmont 8 B2
Denholm 9 E5
Denny 8 A1
Dervaig 10 C2
Dhoon 2 C5
Dingwall 15 H3
Dinnet 16 D6
Dippen 6 D5
Dirleton 9 E1
Distington 3 F4

Dochgarroch 15 H3
Doddington 9 G4
Dollar 8 B1
Dolphinton 8 C3
Donibristle 23 A4
Dores 15 H4
Dornie 14 D4
Dornoch 16 A1
Dougalston 22 B1
Dougarie 6 D5
Douglas *I.o.M.* 2 C6
Douglas *S.Lan.* 8 A4
Douglastown 13 E2
Dounby 21 B2
Doune 12 B4
Dounreay 19 F2
Dowally 12 C2
Dreghorn 7 G5
Drem 9 E2
Drimnin 10 D2
Drongan 7 G6
Druimdrishaig 6 D3
Drumbeg 18 B4
Drumchapel 22 B1
Drumclog 7 H5
Drumlithie 17 F6
Drummore 2 B4
Drumnadrochit 15 H4
Drymen 7 G2
Duchally 18 C5
Duddingston 23 B5
Duddo 9 G3
Dufftown 16 D3
Duirinish 14 D4
Dullatur 22 D1
Dulnain Bridge 16 B4
Dumbarton 7 G3
Dumfries 3 F2
Dunbar 9 E2
Dunbeath 19 G4
Dunblane 12 B4
Dundee 13 E3
Dundonald 7 G5
Dundreggan 15 G5
Dundrennan 3 E3
Dunearn 23 B4
Dunecht 17 F5
Dunfermline 8 B1
Dunkeld 12 C2
Dunlop 7 G4
Dunnet 19 G2
Dunning 12 C4
Dunoon 7 F3
Dunragit 2 B3
Duns 9 F3
Dunscore 3 E1
Duntocher 22 A1
Dunure 7 F6
Dunvegan 14 A3
Durham 4 D3
Durham Tees Valley
　Airport 5 E5
Durness 18 C2
Dyce 17 F5
Dyke 16 B3
Dykehead 13 E1

E
Eaglescliffe 5 E5
Eaglesfield 3 G2
Eaglesham 7 H4
Eaglesham 22 B3
Earlston 9 E4
Earsairidh 20 B10
Easington 5 E3
Easington Colliery 5 E3
East Calder 8 B2
East Haven 13 F3
East Kilbride 7 H4
East Kilbride 22 C3
East Linton 9 E2
East Saltoun 23 D6
East Wemyss 8 D1
Easter Lednathie 13 E1
Easterhouse 22 C2
Eastfield 5 H6
Eastgate 4 C4
Easthouses 23 C6
Eastriggs 3 G2

Ecclaw 9 F2
Ecclefechan 3 G2
Eccles 9 F3
Echt 17 F5
Eckford 9 F4
Edderton 16 A1
Eddleston 8 C3
Edgehead 23 C6
Edinbarnet 22 B1
Edinburgh 8 C2
Edinburgh 23 B5
Edinburgh Airport 8 C2
Edinburgh Airport 23 A5
Edlingham 9 H5
Edmundbyers 4 C3
Edzell 13 F1
Egglescliffe 5 E5
Eglingham 9 H5
Egremont 3 F5
Egton 5 G5
Einacleit 20 D3
Elderslie 22 A2
Elgin 16 D2
Elgol 14 C5
Elie 13 E4
Ellenabeich 6 D1
Ellingham 9 H4
Ellington 4 D1
Ellon 17 G4
Elphin 18 B5
Elphinstone 23 C5
Elsdon 4 C1
Elsrickle 8 B3
Elvanfoot 8 B5
Elvingston 23 D5
Embleton 9 H4
Enterkinfoot 8 A5
Eoropaidh 20 F1
Eriboll 18 C3
Errogie 15 H4
Errol 12 D3
Erskine 22 A1
Esh Winning 4 D3
Eskbank 23 C6
Eskdalemuir 3 G1
Eston 5 F5
Etteridge 15 H6
Ettrick 8 C5
Ettrickbridge 8 D4
Evanton 15 H2
Eyemouth 9 G2

F
Faifley 22 B1
Fairhill 22 D3
Fairholm 22 D3
Fairlie 7 F4
Fairmilehead 23 B6
Fala 23 D6
Fala Dam 23 D6
Falkirk 8 A2
Falkland 12 D4
Fallin 8 A1
Falstone 4 B1
Farr 15 H4
Fauldhouse 8 B2
Fearnmore 14 D2
Felling 4 D2
Felton 9 H5
Fenwick *E.Ayr.* 7 G4
Fenwick *Northumb.* 9 G3
Feochaig 6 D6
Feolin Ferry 6 B3
Ferguslie Park 22 A2
Fern 13 E1
Ferness 16 B3
Ferryden 13 G2
Ferryhill 4 D4
Feshiebridge 16 A5
Fettercairn 13 F1
Finavon 13 E2
Findhorn 16 B2
Findochty 16 D2
Finnygaud 17 E3
Finstown 21 C3
Fintry 7 H2
Fionnphort 10 C3
Fishburn 5 E4
Fishnish 10 D2

Fiunary 10 D2
Flemington 22 C3
Flimby 3 F4
Flodden 9 G4
Fochabers 16 D3
Ford *Arg. & B.* 6 D1
Ford *Midloth.* 23 C6
Fordell 23 A4
Fordoun 13 G1
Fordyce 17 E2
Forfar 13 E2
Forganddenny 12 C4
Forgie 16 D3
Forres 16 B3
Forsinard 19 E3
Fort Augustus 15 G5
Fort William (An Gearasdan) 11 G1
Forth 8 B3
Fortingall 12 B2
Fortrose 16 A3
Foulden 9 G3
Foxbar 22 A2
Foxdale 2 B6
Foyers 15 G4
Fraserburgh 17 G2
Freswick 19 H2
Freuchie 12 D4
Friockheim 13 F2
Frizington 3 F5
Fullwood 22 A3
Furnace 7 E1
Fyvie 17 F4

G
Gabroc Hill 22 A3
Gainford 4 D5
Gairloch 14 D2
Galashiels 8 D4
Gallowhill 22 A2
Galmisdale 14 B6
Galston 7 H5
Gardenstown 17 F2
Garelochhead 7 F2
Garlieston 2 C3
Garsdale Head 4 B6
Gartcosh 22 C2
Gartocharn 7 G2
Garvald 9 E2
Garvamore 15 H6
Garvard 6 B2
Garve 15 G2
Gatehouse of Fleet 2 D3
Gateshead 4 D2
Gawthrop 4 A6
Georgetown 22 A2
Giffnock 7 H4
Giffnock 22 B3
Gifford 9 E2
Gilchriston 23 D6
Gillamoor 5 F6
Gilling West 4 D5
Gilmerton *Edin.* 23 B6
Gilmerton *P. & K.* 12 B3
Gilsland 4 A2
Gilston 8 D3
Girvan 2 B1
Gladsmuir 23 D5
Glamis 13 E2
Glanton 9 G5
Glaschu 22 B2
Glasgow 7 H3
Glasgow 22 B2
Glasgow Airport 7 G3
Glasgow Airport 22 A2
Glasgow Prestwick Airport 7 G5
Glassford 8 A3
Glen Vine 2 C6
Glenbarr 6 C5
Glenbeg 10 D1
Glenboig 22 D2
Glenborrodale 10 D1
Glenbreck 8 B2
Glenbrittle 14 B4
Glenburn 22 A2
Glencaple 3 F2
Glencarse 12 D3

Glencoe 11 G2
Gleneagles 12 C4
Glenegedale 6 B4
Glenelg 14 D5
Glenfarg 12 D4
Glenfinnan 15 E6
Glengarnock 7 G4
Glenkindie 16 D5
Glenluce 2 B3
Glenmavis 22 D2
Glenrothes 12 D4
Gogar 23 A5
Golspie 16 A1
Gordon 9 E3
Gorebridge 8 D2
Gorebridge 23 C6
Gorgie 23 B5
Gosforth *Cumb.* 3 F5
Gosforth *T. & W.* 4 D2
Gourdon 13 G1
Govan 23 B5
Gowkthrapple 22 D3
Grabhair 20 E4
Grandtully 12 C2
Grangemouth 8 B1
Granton 23 B5
Grantown-on-Spey 16 B4
Grantshouse 9 F2
Grasmere 3 H5
Grayrigg 4 A6
Great Ayton 5 F5
Great Broughton 5 F5
Great Clifton 3 F4
Great Salkeld 4 A4
Greenfaulds 22 D1
Greengairs 8 A2
Greengairs 22 D1
Greenhead 4 A2
Greenlaw 9 F3
Greenloaning 12 B4
Greenock 7 F3
Greenodd 3 H6
Gress 20 E2
Gretna 3 H1
Greystoke 3 H4
Grizebeck 3 G6
Grudie 15 G2
Guide Post 4 D1
Guildtown 12 D3
Guisborough 5 F5
Gullane 8 D1
Gullane 23 D4
Gutcher 21 J2

H
Hackness 5 H6
Haddington 9 E2
Haggs 22 D1
Halbeath 23 A4
Halket 22 A3
Halkirk 19 G3
Hall 7 G4
Hall 22 A3
Haltwhistle 4 B2
Ham 21 F5
Hamilton 8 A3
Hamilton 22 D3
Hamnavoe (Mainland) 21 H5
Harbost 20 F1
Haroldswick 21 J1
Harrietfield 12 C3
Harthill 8 B2
Hartlepool 5 F4
Hassendean 9 E4
Haswell 5 E3
Hatton 17 G4
Haugh of Urr 3 E2
Haughhead 22 C1
Hawes 4 B6
Hawick 9 E5
Hawkshead 3 H6
Haydon Bridge 4 B2
Healeyfield 4 C3
Hebburn 5 E2
Helensburgh 7 F2
Helmsdale 19 F1
Helmsley 5 F6
Heriot 8 D3

Hermiston 23 A5
Hetton-le-Hole 5 E3
Hexham 4 C2
High Blantyre 7 H4
High Blantyre 22 C3
High Etherley 4 D4
High Hawsker 5 H5
High Hesket 3 H3
High Lorton 3 G4
Hill End 8 B1
Hill of Fearn 16 A2
Hillend *Fife* 23 A4
Hillend *Midloth.* 23 B6
Hillington 22 B2
Hillside 13 G1
Hillswick 21 H3
Hinderwell 5 G5
Hollybush 7 G6
Holytown 22 D2
Holywood 3 F1
Hopeman 16 C2
Horden 5 E3
Horsehouse 4 C6
Hoswick 21 H5
Houghton le Spring 5 E3
Houndslow 9 E3
Houston 7 G3
Houston 22 A2
Houton 21 C3
Howmood 7 G3
Howwood 22 A2
Huisinis 20 C4
Humbie 8 D2
Humbie 23 D6
Hunter's Quay 7 F3
Huntly 17 E3
Hurlford 7 G5
Hurworth-on-Tees 5 E5
Hutton Rudby 5 E5

I
Idrigil 14 B2
Inchbare 13 F1
Inchinnan 22 A2
Inchnadamph 18 B4
Inchture 12 D3
Ingleton 4 B6
Ingliston 23 A5
Innellan 7 F3
Innerleithen 8 D4
Insch 17 E4
Inveralligin 14 D3
Inverallochy 17 G2
Inveraray 7 E1
Inverarity 13 E2
Inverarnan 7 G1
Inverbervie 13 G1
Invercassley 18 C5
Invercharnan 11 G2
Inveresk 23 C5
Inverey 16 B6
Invergarry 15 G5
Invergordon 16 A2
Inverinan 7 E1
Inverkeilor 13 F2
Inverkeithing 8 C1
Inverkeithing 23 A4
Inverkirkaig 18 A5
Inverlael 15 F1
Invermoriston 15 G5
Inverneil 6 D2
Inverness (Inbhir Nis) 16 A3
Inverness Airport 16 A3
Invernoaden 7 F2
Inverurie 17 F4
Irvine 7 G5
Islay Airport 6 B4
Isle of Man Airport 2 B6
Isle of Whithorn 2 C4

J
Jackton 22 B3
Jarrow 5 E2
Jedburgh 9 E4
Jemimaville 16 A2
John o' Groats 19 H2
Johnstone 7 G3
Johnstone 22 A2

Johnstone Castle 22 A2
Johnstonebridge 3 F1
Juniper Green 23 A6

K
Kaimes 23 B6
Kames 7 E3
Keillmore 6 C2
Keiss 19 H2
Keith 16 D3
Kellas *Angus* 13 E3
Kellas *Moray* 16 C3
Kelso 9 F4
Kelty 8 C1
Kelvinside 22 B2
Kemnay 17 F5
Kendal 4 A6
Kenknock 11 H3
Kenmore 12 B2
Kennacraig 6 D3
Kennethmont 17 E4
Kennoway 13 E4
Kensaleyre 14 B3
Kentallen 11 F2
Keoldale 18 C2
Keswick 3 G4
Kielder 4 A1
Kilbarchan 22 A2
Kilberry 6 D3
Kilbirnie 7 G4
Kilcadzow 8 A3
Kilchattan 7 F4
Kilchenzie 6 C5
Kilchiaran 6 A4
Kilchoan 10 C1
Kilchoman 6 A3
Kilchrenan 11 F3
Kilconquhar 13 E4
Kilcreggan 7 F2
Kildonan Lodge 19 F4
Kildrummy 16 D5
Kilfinan 7 E3
Kilham 9 F4
Killean 6 C4
Killearn 7 H2
Killichonan 12 A2
Killiecrankie 12 C1
Killin 12 A3
Killingworth 4 D2
Killundine 10 D2
Kilmacolm 7 G3
Kilmalieu 11 E2
Kilmaluag 14 B2
Kilmarnock 7 G5
Kilmartin 7 E1
Kilmaurs 7 G4
Kilmelford 6 D1
Kilmeny 6 B3
Kilmorack 16 A3
Kilmory *Arg. & B.* 6 D3
Kilmory *High.* 14 B5
Kilninian 10 C2
Kilninver 11 E3
Kiloran 6 B2
Kilrenny 13 F4
Kilsyth 8 A2
Kilsyth 22 D1
Kilwinning 7 G4
Kinbrace 19 F4
Kincardine 8 B1
Kincardine O'Neil 17 E6
Kincraig 16 A5
Kingarth 7 E4
Kinghorn 8 C1
Kinghorn 23 B4
Kinglassie 8 C1
Kingsbarns 13 F4
Kingshouse 12 A3
Kingston 16 D2
Kingussie 16 A5
Kinkell 22 C1
Kinloch 14 B6
Kinloch Hourn 15 E5
Kinloch Rannoch 12 A2
Kinlochard 7 G1
Kinlochbervie 18 B3
Kinlochell 11 F1
Kinlochewe 15 E2
Kinlochleven 11 G1
Kinloss 16 B2
Kinross 12 D4

Kintore 17 F5
Kintour 9 F5
Kintra 6 B4
Kippen 7 H2
Kirk Michael 2 C5
Kirk Yetholm 9 F4
Kirkbean 3 F3
Kirkbride 3 G3
Kirkby Stephen 4 B5
Kirkbymoorside 5 F6
Kirkcaldy 8 C1
Kirkcolm 2 A2
Kirkconnel 8 A5
Kirkcowan 2 C2
Kirkcudbright 2 D3
Kirkinner 2 C3
Kirkintilloch 7 H3
Kirkintilloch 22 C1
Kirkliston 8 C1
Kirkliston 23 A5
Kirkmichael *P. & K.* 12 C1
Kirkmichael *S.Ayr.* 7 G6
Kirkmuirhill 8 A3
Kirknewton *Northumb.* 9 G4
Kirknewton *W.Loth.* 8 C2
Kirknewton *W.Loth.* 23 A6
Kirkoswald *Cumb.* 4 A3
Kirkoswald *S.Ayr.* 7 F6
Kirkpatrick Durham 3 E2
Kirkpatrick-Fleming 3 G2
Kirkton 6 D1
Kirkton of Culsalmond 17 E4
Kirkton of Durris 17 F6
Kirkton of Glenisla 12 D1
Kirkton of Kingoldrum 13 E2
Kirkton of Menmuir 13 F1
Kirkton of Skene 17 F5
Kirktown of Auchterless 17 F3
Kirktown of Deskford 17 E2
Kirkwall 21 C3
Kirkwall Airport 21 C3
Kirriemuir 13 E2
Knayton 5 E6
Knightswood 22 B2
Knock 10 D3
Knockandhu 16 C4
Kyle of Lochalsh (Caol Loch Aillse) 14 D4
Kyleakin 14 D4
Kylerhea 14 D4
Kyles Scalpay 20 D5
Kylestrome 18 B4

L
Ladybank 12 D4
Ladykirk 9 F3
Ladysford 17 G2
Lagg 7 H2
Laggan (Invergarry) *High.* 15 F6
Laggan (Newtonmore) *High.* 15 H6
Lagganulva 10 C2
Laide 14 D1
Lairg 18 D5
Lamlash 7 E5
Lanark 8 A3
Lanchester 4 D3
Langholm 3 H1
Langside 22 B2
Langwathby 4 A4
Larbert 8 A1
Largoward 13 E4
Largs 7 F4
Larkhall 8 A3
Larkhall 22 D3
Lasswade 23 C6
Latheron 19 G4
Latheronwheel 19 G4

Rattray 12 D2
Ravenglass 3 F6
Rawyards 22 D2
Reay 19 F2
Red Point 14 D2
Redcar 5 F4
Redcastle 15 H3
Redford 13 F2
Reiff 18 A5
Reiss 19 H3
Renfrew 7 H3
Renfrew 22 B2
Rennington 9 H5
Rescobie 13 F2
Reston 9 F2
Rhiconich 18 B3
Rhu 7 F2
Rhynie 16 D4
Richmond 4 D5
Rickarton 17 F6
Riding Mill 4 C2
Riggend 22 D2
Rigside 8 A4
Ringford 2 D3
Roadside 19 G2
Roadside of
      Kinneff 13 G1
Roberton *Sc.Bord.* 8 D5
Roberton *S.Lan.* 8 B4
Robin Hood's Bay 5 H5
Rochester 4 B1
Rockcliffe 3 E3
Rodel 20 C5
Rogart 19 E5
Romannobridge 8 C3
Rosedale Abbey 5 G6
Rosehearty 17 G2
Rosemarkie 16 A3
Rosewell 8 C2
Rosewell 23 B6
Roshven 11 E1
Roskhill 14 A3
Roslin 8 C2
Roslin 23 B6
Rothbury 9 G5
Rothes 16 C3
Rothesay 7 E3
Rowlands Gill 4 D3
Roybridge 15 F6
Rutherend 22 C3
Rutherglen 7 H3
Rutherglen 22 C2

S

Sacriston 4 D3
Saddell 6 D5
Saighdinis 20 B6
St. Abbs 9 G2
St. Andrews 13 F4
St. Bees 3 F5
St. Combs 17 G2
St. Cyrus 13 G1
St. Davids 23 A4
St. Fergus 17 H3
St. Fillans 12 A3
St. John's Chapel 4 B4
St. John's Town of
      Dalry 2 D1
St. Margaret's Hope 21 C4
St. Mary's 21 C3
St. Monans 13 F4
Salen *Arg. & B.* 10 D2
Salen *High.* 10 D1
Saline 8 B1
Salsburgh 8 A2
Saltburn-by-the-Sea 5 F4
Saltcoats 7 F4
Samuelston 23 D5
Sanaigmore 6 A3
Sandgarth 21 D3
Sandhead 2 A3
Sandness 21 G4
Sandsend 5 G5
Sandwick 21 H5
Sandygate 2 C5
Sanquhar 8 A5
Satley 4 D3
Scalasaig 6 B2

Scalby 5 H6
Scalloway 21 H5
Scarborough 5 H6
Scardroy 15 F3
Scarinish 10 A2
Scone 12 D3
Sconser 14 C4
Scorton 4 D5
Scotch Corner 4 D5
Scotstoun 22 B2
Scotton 4 D6
Scourie 18 B3
Scousburgh 21 H6
Scrabster 19 F2
Scremerston 9 G3
Seaham 5 E3
Seahouses 9 H4
Seamer 5 H6
Seamill 7 F4
Seascale 3 F5
Seaton 3 F4
Seaton Delaval 5 E2
Seaton Sluice 5 E2
Sedbergh 4 A6
Sedgefield 5 E4
Seghill 4 D2
Selkirk 8 D4
Sellafield 3 F5
Sgiogarstaigh 20 F1
Shap 4 A5
Shawbost 20 D2
Sherburn 5 E3
Shettleston 22 C2
Shiel Bridge 15 E5
Shieldaig 14 D3
Shilbottle 9 H5
Shildon 4 D4
Shinness Lodge 18 D5
Shiremoor 5 E2
Shotts 8 A2
Silloth 3 G3
Silverburn 23 B6
Skaill (West Coast) 21 B3
Skeld 21 H4
Skelmorlie 7 F3
Skelton 5 F5
Skelwick 21 C1
Skerray 18 D2
Skipness 7 E4
Slamannan 8 A2
Sleights 5 G5
Sligachan 14 B4
Smailholm 9 E4
Smnaiton 5 H6
Sollas 20 B6
Sorbie 2 C3
Sorisdale 10 B1
Sorn 7 H5
South Bank 5 F4
South Gyle 23 A5
South Hetton 5 E3
South Queensferry
      (Queensferry) 8 C2
**South Queensferry
      (Queensferry) 23 A5**
South Shields 5 E2
Southbar 22 A2
Southdean 9 E5
Southend 6 C6
Sowerby 5 E6
Spean Bridge 15 F6
Spennymoor 4 D4
Spey Bay 16 D2
Spinningdale 15 H1
Spittal *E.Loth.* 23 D5
Spittal *High.* 19 G3
Spittal of Glenshee 12 D1
Springburn 22 C2
Springholm 3 E2
Springside 7 G5
Sproxton 5 F6
Staffin 14 B2
Staindrop 4 D4
Staintondale 5 H6
Stalling Busk 4 C6
Stamfordham 4 C2
Stand 22 D2
Stane 8 A3
Stanhope 4 C4

Stanley *Dur.* 4 D3
Stanley *P. & K.* 12 D3
Stannington 5 D2
Startforth 4 C5
Stenhousemuir 8 A1
Stenton 9 E2
Stepps 22 C2
Stevenston 7 F4
Stewarton 7 G4
Stichill 9 F4
Stilligarry 20 B8
Stirling 8 A1
Stobo 8 C4
Stocksfield 4 C2
Stockton-on-Tees 5 E4
Stoer 18 A4
Stokesley 5 F5
Stonehaven 17 F6
Stonehouse 8 A3
Stoneykirk 2 A3
Stonybreck 21 F6
Stornoway
      (Steornabhagh) 20 E3
Stornoway Airport 20 E3
Stow 8 D3
Strachan 17 E6
Strachur 7 F1
Straiton 23 B6
Straloch 12 C1
Stranraer 2 A2
Strathaven 8 A3
Strathblane 7 H3
Strathblane 22 B1
Strathdon 16 D5
Strathmiglo 12 D4
Strathpeffer 15 G3
Strathy 19 E2
Strathyre 7 H1
Strichen 17 G3
Stromeferry 14 D4
Stromness 21 B3
Stronachlachar 7 G1
Strone 7 F2
Strontian 11 E1
Stuartfield 17 G3
Sumburgh 21 H6
Sumburgh Airport 21 H6
Sunderland 5 E3
Swanston 23 B6
Swinton 9 F3
Symbister 21 J3
Symington *S.Ayr.* 7 G5
Symington *S.Lan.* 8 B4
Syre 18 D3

T

Tain 16 A1
Talisker 14 B4
Talladale 15 E2
Talmine 18 D2
Tannadice 13 E2
Tannochside 22 C2
Tarbert (Kintyre)
      Arg. & B. 6 D3
Tarbert (Jura)
      Arg. & B. 6 C2
Tarbert (An Tairbeart)
      W.Isles 20 D4
Tarbet 7 G1
Tarbolton 7 G5
Tarfside 16 D6
Tarrel 16 A1
Tarves 17 F4
Tayinloan 6 C4
Taynuilt 11 F3
Tayport 13 E3
Tayvallich 6 D2
Tealing 13 E3
Teangue 14 C5
Tebay 4 A5
Temple Sowerby 4 A4
Teviothead 8 D5
The Murray 22 C3
Thirsk 5 E6
Thornaby-on-Tees 5 E5
Thornhill *D. & G.* 3 E1
Thornhill *Stir.* 7 H1
Thornley 5 E4
Thornliebank 22 B3

Thornton 8 C1
Thorntonhall 22 B3
Thornton-le-Dale 5 G6
Threlkeld 3 H4
Thropton 9 G5
Thrumster 19 H3
Thursby 3 H3
Thurso (Inbhir
      Theòrsa) 19 G2
Thwaite 4 B6
Tibbermore 12 C3
Tighnabruaich 7 E3
Tillicoultry 8 B1
Tillyfourie 17 E5
Timsgearraidh 20 C3
Tingwall 21 C2
Tiree Airport 10 A2
Toab 21 H6
Tobermory 10 D2
Toberonochy 6 D1
Togston 9 H5
Tolastadh Úr 20 F2
Toll of Birness 17 G4
Tollcross 22 C2
Tomatin 16 A4
Tomich 15 H2
Tomintoul 16 C5
Tomnavoulin 16 C4
Tongland 3 E3
Tongue 18 D3
Tore 15 H3
Tormore 17 E5
Torphichen 8 B2
Torphins 17 E5
Torrance 7 H3
Torrance 22 C1
Torrance House 22 C3
Torridon 14 D3
Torrin 14 C4
Torthorwald 3 F2
Torver 3 G6
Toscaig 14 D4
Tow Law 4 D4
Town Yetholm 9 F4
Townhead of
      Greenlaw 3 E2
Townhill 23 A4
Tranent 8 D2
Tranent 23 D5
Tressait 12 B1
Trimdon 5 E4
Trinity *Angus* 13 F1
Trinity *Edin.* 23 B5
Trochry 12 C2
Troon 7 G5
Troutbeck 3 H5
Troutbeck Bridge 3 H5
Tummel Bridge 12 B2
Turnberry 7 F6
Turriff 17 F3
Twechar 7 H3
Twechar 22 D1
Tweedmouth 9 G3
Tweedsmuir 8 B4
Twynholm 2 D3
Tyndrum 11 H3
Tynemouth 5 E2

U

Uachdar 20 B7
Uddingston 7 H3
Uddingston 22 C2
Uddington 8 A4
Udston 22 D3
Uig (Uige) 14 B2
Ulbster 19 H3
Ulgham 4 D1
Ullapool (Ullapul) 15 F1
Ulpha 3 G6
Ulsta 21 H2
Unapool 18 B4
Uplawmoor 22 A3
Upper Knockando 16 C3
Ushaw Moor 4 D3
Uyeasound 21 J1

V

Valsgarth 21 J1
Veensgarth 21 H4

Vidlin 21 H3
Viewpark 22 D2
Voe 21 H3

W

Walls 21 G4
Wallsend 5 E2
Wallyford 23 C5
Warcop 4 B5
Wark 4 B2
Warkworth 9 H5
Warwick Bridge 3 H3
Washington 5 E3
Watchgate 4 A6
Waterbeck 3 G2
Waterfoot 22 B3
Waterside 22 C1
Watten 19 G3
Wattston 22 D2
Weem 12 B2
Weisdale 21 H4
Wemyss Bay 7 F3
Wensley 4 C6
West Auckland 4 D4
West Calder 8 B2
West Carbeth 22 B1
West Kilbride 7 F4
West Linton 8 C3
West Saltoun 23 D6
West Sandwick 21 H2
West Tarbert 6 D3
Wester Hailes 23 B6
Westerdale 19 G3
Westfield 22 D1
Westgate 4 C4
Westhill 17 F5
Westnewton 3 G3
Westruther 9 E3
Westwood 22 C3
Wetheral 3 H3
Whalton 4 D1
Whauphill 2 C3
Wheatley Hill 5 E4
Whickham 4 D2
Whifflet 22 D2
Whitburn 8 B2
Whitby 5 G5
Whitecraig 8 D2
Whitecraig 23 C5
Whitehall 21 D2
Whitehaven 3 F5
Whitehill 23 C6
Whitehills 17 E2
Whiteness 21 H4
Whiterashes 17 F4
Whithorn 2 C3
Whiting Bay 7 E5
Whitley Bay 5 E2
Whittingham 9 G5
Wick 19 H3
Wick Airport 19 H3
Wigton 3 G3
Wigtown 2 C3
Wilkieston 23 A6
Willington 4 D4
Winchburgh 8 B2
Windermere 3 H6
Windygates 13 E4
Windy-Yett 22 A3
Wingate 5 E4
Winston 4 D5
Winton 4 B5
Wishaw 8 A3
Wishaw 22 D3
Witton Gilbert 4 D3
Wolsingham 4 C4
Woodland 4 C4
Wooler 9 G4
Workington 3 F4
Wormit 13 E3
Wrelton 5 G6

Y

Yarm 5 E5
Yarrow 8 D4
Yetts o' Muckhart 12 C4
Yoker 22 B2

M8	Motorway / under construction or proposed
A82 ❶	Primary route dual / single carriageway / Junction
A70	'A' Road dual / single
B793	'B' Road dual / single
Toll	Other road dual / single carriageway / Toll
→	One way street
	Access restriction
	Pedestrian street
	Minor road / Track
	Railway line / station
	Light Rail / Station
	Light Rail under construction
	Railway tunnel / Level crossing
P	Bus (Coach) station / Car Park
	Leisure & tourism
	Shopping
	Administration & law
	Education
	Health & welfare
	Industry & Commerce
	Other notable building
PO	Post Office
Pol Lib	Police station / Library
Hilton	Major Hotel
	Cinema / Theatre
	Tourist information centre (all year / seasonal)
	Toilet
+ ☽ ✡	Church / Mosque / Synagogue
■	Fire station / Ambulance station / Community centre

Abbreviations used in town plan indexes

All	Alley
App	Approach
Arc	Arcade
Av	Avenue
Bk	Bank
Bldgs	Buildings
Boul	Boulevard
Bri	Bridge
Cen	Central/Centre
Cft	Croft
Ch	Church
Circ	Circus
Clo	Close
Coll	College
Cor	Corner
Cotts	Cottages
Cres	Crescent
Ct	Court
Dr	Drive
E	East
Esp	Esplanade
Est	Estate
Ex	Exchange
Fm	Farm
Gdn	Garden
Gdns	Gardens
Gra	Grange
Grn	Green
Gro	Grove
Hts	Heights
Ho	House
Hos	Hospital
Ind	Industrial
Junct	Junction
La	Lane
Lit	Loan
Mans	Mansion
Mkt	Market
Ms	Mews
Mt	Mount
N	North
Par	Parade
Pk	Park
Pl	Place
Quad	Quadrant
Rd	Road
Ri	Rise
S	South
Sch	School
Sq	Square
St	Street
St.	Saint
Sta	Station
Ter	Terrace
Twr	Tower
Vills	Villas
Vw	View
W	West
Wd	Wood
Wds	Woods
Wf	Wharf
Wk	Walk
Wks	Works
Yd	Yard

ABERDEEN

Maps 30-33 Index 34-35
Scale 4 inches to 1 mile

EDINBURGH

Maps 36-45 Index 46-51
Scale 4 inches to 1 mile
City centre map 5.7 inches to 1 mile

GLASGOW

Maps 52-59 Index 60-66
Scale 4 inches to 1 mile

Dundee map & index 67
Inverness map & index 68
Perth map & index 69

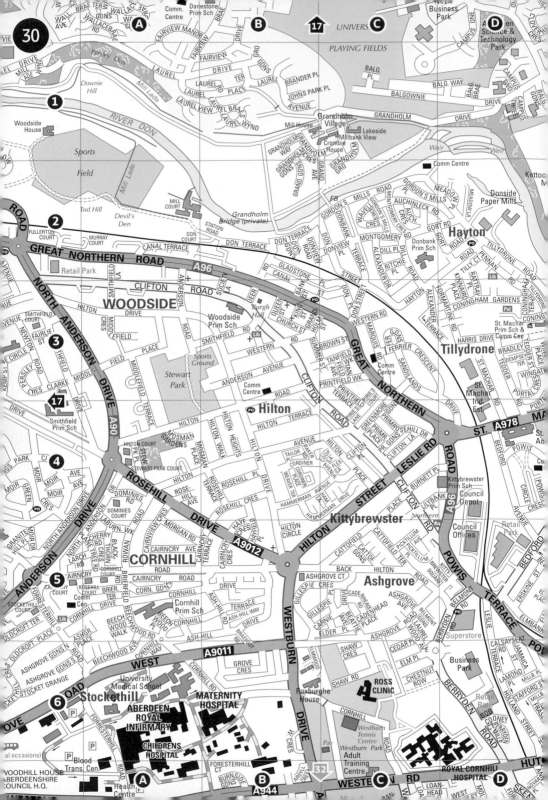

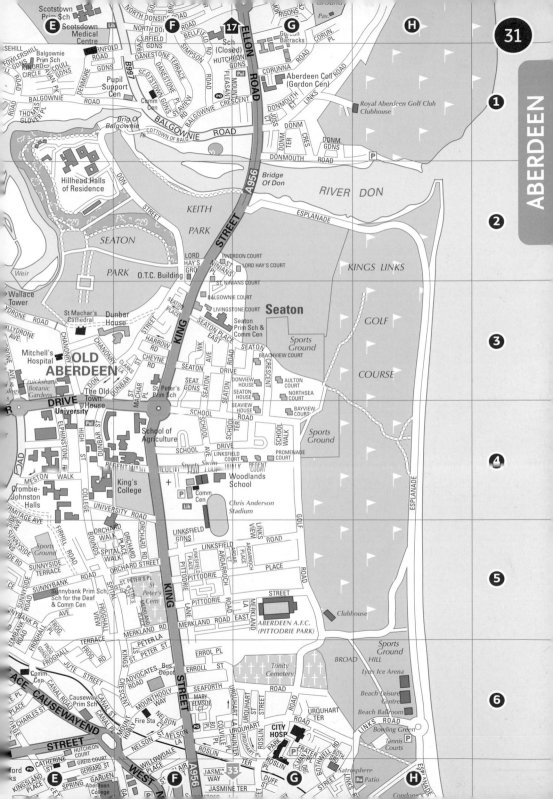

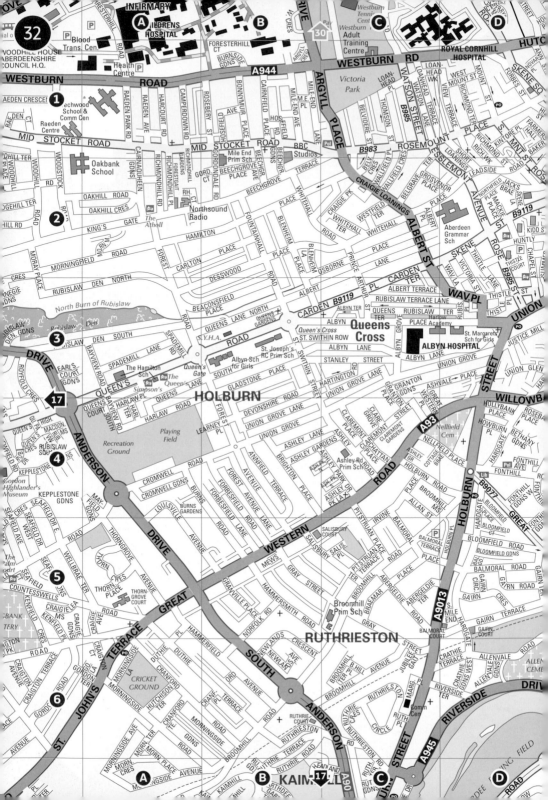

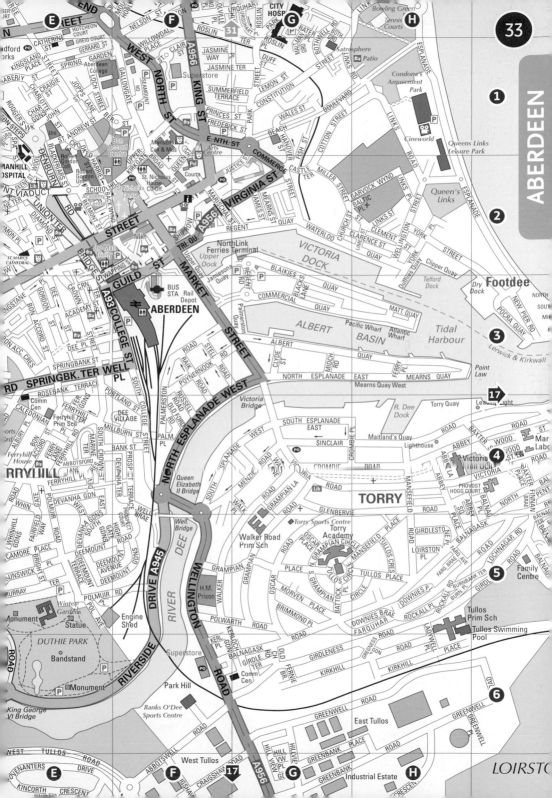

A

Street	Page	Grid
Abbey La	33	H4
Abbey Pl	33	H4
Abbey Rd	33	H4
Abbey Sq	33	H4
Abbotsford La	33	E4
Abergeldie Rd	32	C5
Abergeldie Ter	32	C5
Academy St	33	E3
Advocates Rd	31	F6
Albert La	32	B3
Albert Pl	32	C2
Albert Quay	33	G3
Albert St	32	C2
Albert Ter	32	C3
Albury La	33	E4
Albury Rd	32	D4
Albyn Gro	32	C3
Albyn La	32	C3
Albyn Pl	32	C3
Albyn Ter	32	C3
Alexander Dr	30	C2
Alexander Ter	30	C3
Allan St	32	C3
Allenvale Gdns	32	D6
Allenvale Rd	32	D6
Anderson Av	30	B3
Anderson Rd	30	A2
Annfield Ter	32	B4
Ann St	32	D1
Ardarroch Pl	31	G5
Ardarroch Rd	31	F5
Argyll Cres	32	B1
Argyll Pl	32	B1
Ashgrove Av	30	C5
Ashgrove Ct	30	B5
Ashgrove Rd	30	C5
Ash-hill Dr	30	A5
Ash-hill Rd	30	B5
Ash-hill Way	30	B5
Ashley Gdns	32	B4
Ashley Gro	32	C4
Ashley La	32	B4
Ashley Pk Dr	32	B4
Ashley Pk La	32	C4
Ashley Pk N	32	B4
Ashley Pk S	32	C4
Ashley Rd	32	C4
Ashvale Pl	32	C3
Auchinleck Cres	30	C2
Auchinleck Ct	30	C2
Aulton Ct	31	G3

B

Street	Page	Grid
Back Hilton Rd	30	C5
Back Wynd	33	E2
Baker St	32	D1
Balgownie Brae	31	F3
Balgownie Cres	31	F1
Balgownie Dr	30	C1
Balgownie Gdns	30	D1
Balgownie Pl	30	C1
Balgownie Rd	31	F1
Balgownie Way	30	C1
Balmoral Ct	32	C5
Balmoral Pl	32	C5
Balmoral Rd	32	D5
Balmoral Ter	32	C5
Balnagask Rd	33	H5
Baltic Pl	33	H2
Baltic St	33	G2
Bank St	33	E4
Bank St (Woodside)	30	B3
Battock Pl	33	G5
Baxter St	33	H4
Bayview Ct	31	G4
Bayview Rd	32	A3
Bayview Rd S	32	A4
Beach Boul	33	G3
Beachview Ct	31	G3
Beaconsfield Pl	32	A3
Beattie Av	30	C5
Bedford Av	30	D4
Bedford Pl	30	D5
Bedford Rd	30	D5
Beechgrove Av	32	B2
Beechgrove Gdns	32	B1
Beechgrove Pl	32	B2
Beechgrove Ter	32	B2
Beechwood Av	30	A6
Beechwood Pl	30	A5
Beechwood Rd	30	A5
Beechwood Wk	30	A5
Belgrave Ter	32	C2
Belmont Gdns	30	C5
Belmont Rd	30	D5
Belmont St	33	E2
Belvidere Cres	32	C2
Belvidere St	32	C1
Berryden Rd	30	D6
Berry St	33	F1
Bethany Gdns	32	B3
Blackfriars St	33	E1
Blacks La	33	G3
Blackthorn Cres	30	A5
Blaikies Quay	33	G2
Blenheim La	32	B2
Blenheim Pl	32	B2
Bloomfield Ct	32	D5
Bloomfield Pl	32	D4
Bloomfield Rd	32	D5
Bob Cooney Ct	30	D6
Boddie Pl	31	F6
Bon Accord Cres	33	E3
Bon Accord St	33	E3
Bonnymuir Pl	32	B1
Bradley Ter	30	D3
Braefoot Rd	30	D3
Braemar Pl	32	C5
Brander Pl	30	B1
Bridge of Don	31	G2
Bridge St	33	E2
Brierfield Rd	30	A5
Brighton Pl	32	B4
Bright St	33	E5
Brig o' Balgownie	31	F1
Brimmond Pl	33	G5
Broomhill Av	32	C6
Broomhill Pl	32	C5
Broomhill Rd	32	C5
Broomhill Ter	32	C6
Brown St	30	C3
Brunswick Pl	33	E5
Burnbank Pl	33	H5
Burnbank Ter	33	H5
Burnett Pl	30	C4
Burns Gdns	32	A4
Burnside Gdns	32	B1
Burns Rd	32	A4

C

Street	Page	Grid
Cadenhead Pl	30	C5
Cadenhead Rd	30	C5
Cairnaquheen Gdns	32	A1
Cairncry Av	30	A5
Cairncry Cres	30	B5
Cairncry Rd	30	A5
Cairncry Ter	30	A5
Cairnfield Pl	32	B1
Cairnfield Rd	31	E1
Cairnview Cres	30	A5
Caledonian Pl	33	E4
Calsayseat Rd	30	D6
Camperdown Rd	32	A1
Campus One	30	D1
Campus Three	30	D1
Campus Two	30	D1
Canal Pl	31	E6
Canal Rd	31	E6
Canal St	31	E6
Canal St (Woodside)	30	B2
Canal Ter	30	A2
Carden Pl	32	B3
Carden Ter	32	C3
Carlton Pl	32	A2
Carnie Dr	30	B5
Castle Ter	33	G2
Catherine St	33	E1
Cattofield Gdns	30	C5
Cattofield Pl	30	C5
Cattofield Ter	30	C5
Causewayend	31	E6
Cedar Pl	30	C6
Chanonry	31	E3
Chapel St	32	D2
Charles St	31	E6
Charlotte Gdns	33	E1
Charlotte St	33	E1
Chattan Pl	32	C4
Cherry Rd	30	A5
Chestnut Row	30	C6
Cheyne Rd	31	F3
Church St	33	G2
Church St (Woodside)	30	B3
Claremont Gdns	32	C4
Claremont Gro	32	C4
Claremont Pl	32	C4
Claremont St	32	C4
Clarence St	33	G2
Clarks La	31	F3
Clifton La	30	C4
Clifton Pl	30	C4
Clifton Rd	30	A3
Clyde St	33	G3
College Bounds	31	E4
College St	33	E3
Colville Pl	31	F6
Commerce St	33	F1
Commercial Quay	33	G3
Coningham Gdns	30	D3
Coningham Rd	30	D3
Coningham Ter	30	D3
Constitution St	33	G1
Cornhill Ct	30	A5
Cornhill Dr	30	A5
Cornhill Gdns	30	A5
Cornhill Rd	30	A6
Cornhill Ter	30	A6
Cornhill Way	30	A6
Corsehill Gdns	30	D1
Corunna Rd	31	G1
Cottage Brae	32	C4
Cotton St	33	G1
Cottown of Balgownie	31	F1
Coull Gdns	31	E1
Craigielea Av	32	A5
Craigie Loanings	32	C2
Craigie Pk	32	C2
Craigie St	33	E1
Craigton Ct	32	A6
Cranford Pl	32	A6
Cranford Rd	32	A6
Cranford Ter	32	A6
Crathie Gdns W	32	D6
Crathie Ter	32	C6
Crimon Pl	33	E2
Crombie Pl	33	G4
Crombie Rd	33	G4
Cromwell Gdns	32	A4
Cromwell Rd	32	A4
Crooked La	33	E1
Crown St	33	E3
Crown Ter	33	E3

D

Street	Page	Grid
Danestone Pl	31	F1
Danestone Ter	31	F1
Davan Pk	31	E1
Deemount Av	33	E5
Deemount Gdns	33	E5
Deemount Rd	33	E5
Deemount Ter	33	E5
Dee Pl	33	E3
Deer Rd	30	B3
Dee St	33	E3
Dempsey Ct	30	D3
Denburn Rd	33	E1
Denmore Gdns	31	E1
Desswood Pl	32	B3
Devanha Cres	33	E4
Devanha Gdns	33	E4
Devanha Gdns E	33	E4
Devanha Gdns S	33	E4
Devanha Gdns W	33	E4
Devanha Ter	33	E4
Devonshire Rd	32	B4
Diamond St	33	E2
Dill Pl	30	C2
Dill Rd	30	C2
Dominies Ct	30	A4
Dominies Rd	30	A4
Donbank Ter	30	C2
Don Ct	30	A2
Don Gdns	30	B2
Donmouth Ct	31	G1
Donmouth Cres	31	G1
Donmouth Gdns	31	G1
Donmouth Rd	31	G1
Donmouth Ter	31	G1
Don Pl	30	C3
Don St (Old Aberdeen)	31	E3
Don St (Woodside)	30	C3
Don Ter	30	B2
Donview Ho	31	G3
Donview Pl	30	C2
Donview Rd	30	B2
Downies Brae	33	G5
Downies Pl	33	H5
Duff St	33	G1
Dunbar St	31	E4
Duthie Pl	32	A6
Duthie Ter	32	A6

E

Street	Page	Grid
East N St	33	F1
East Tullos Ind Est	33	H6
Elder Rd	30	B5
Elmbank Rd	31	E6
Elmbank Ter	30	D5
Elmfield Av	30	D5
Elmfield Pl	30	D5
Elmfield Ter	30	D5
Elm Pl	30	C6
Elphinstone Rd	31	E4
Errol Pl	31	F6
Errol St	31	F6
Erskine St	30	D5
Esplanade	33	H2
Esslemont Av	32	C1
Exchange St	33	F2

F

Street	Page	Grid
Fairview Brae	30	A1
Fairview Dr	30	B1
Farmers Hall La	32	D1
Farquhar Av	33	H5
Farquhar Brae	33	H5
Farquhar Rd	33	H5
Fernie Brae	33	G6
Ferrier Cres	30	C3
Ferrier Gdns	30	C3
Ferryhill Gdns	33	E4
Ferryhill La	33	E4
Ferryhill Pl	33	E4
Ferryhill Rd	33	E4
Ferryhill Ter	33	E4
Ferry Pl	33	H3
Firhill Rd	31	E5
Fish St	33	G2
Fonthill Gdns E	32	D5
Fonthill Gdns W	32	D4
Fonthill Rd	32	D4
Fonthill Ter	32	D4
Forbesfield La	32	B4
Forbesfield Rd	32	B4
Forbes St	32	D1
Forest Av	32	B4
Forest Av La	32	B4
Foresterhill Ct	32	B1
Forestgait	32	A2
Forest Rd	32	A2
Formartine Rd	30	C3
Forresterhill Rd	30	A6
Fountainhall Rd	32	B2
Fowlershill Gdns	31	E1
Fraser Ct	31	E6
Fraserfield Gdns	31	F1
Fraser Pl	30	D6
Fraser Rd	30	D6
Fraser St	30	D6
Frederick St	33	F1
Froghall Av	31	E6
Froghall Gdns	31	E6
Froghall Pl	31	E5
Froghall Rd	31	E6
Froghall Ter	31	E6
Froghall Vw	31	E5

G

Street	Page	Grid
Gairn Circle	32	D5
Gairn Ct	32	D5
Gairn Cres	32	D5
Gairn Rd	32	D5
Gairn Ter	32	D5
Gallowgate	33	F1
Garvock Wynd	33	H2
George St	31	E6
Gerrard St	33	E1
Gilcomston Steps	32	D1
Gillespie Cres	30	B5
Gillespie Pl	30	B5
Girdleness Rd	33	H5
Girdleness Ter	33	G6
Girdlestone Pl	33	H5
Gladstone Pl	32	B3
Gladstone Pl (Woodside)	30	B2
Glenbervie Rd	33	G4
Golf Rd	31	G5
Gordondale Ct	32	A2
Gordondale Rd	32	B1
Gordon La	32	A6
Gordon's Mills Cres	30	C2
Gordon's Mills Pl	30	C2
Gordon's Mills Rd	30	C2
Gordon St	33	E3
Gort Rd	30	C2
Grampian La	33	G4
Grampian Pl	33	F5
Grampian Rd	33	G5
Grandholm Br (Private)	30	B2
Grandholm St	30	B3
Granton Pl	32	C3
Granville Pl	32	B5
Gray St	32	B5
Gray St Ms	32	B5
Great Northern Rd	30	C3
Great Southern Rd	32	D5
Great Western Pl	32	C4
Great Western Rd	32	A5
Greenmore Gdns	33	H6
Greenwell Pl	33	H6
Greenwell Rd	33	H6
Gregness Gdns	33	H6
Greig Ct	33	E1
Grosvenor Pl	32	C2
Grove Cres	30	B6
Guild St	33	F3

H

Street	Page	Grid
Hamilton Pl	32	A2
Hammerfield Av	32	A5
Hammersmith Rd	32	B5
Hanover St	33	G1
Harcourt Rd	32	A1
Hardgate	32	D4
Harlaw Pl	32	A4
Harlaw Rd	32	A4
Harlaw Ter	32	A4
Harriet St	33	E2
Harris Dr	30	D3
Harrow Rd	31	F3
Hartington Rd	32	B3
Hayfield Cres	30	B5
Hayfield Pl	30	B4
Hayton Rd	30	C3
Hermitage Av	31	E4
Highgate Gdns	33	F5
High St	31	E4
Hill St	32	D1
Hill Vw Gdns	33	G6
Hillview Rd	33	G6
Hilton Av	30	A4
Hilton Circle	30	B5
Hilton Ct	30	A4
Hilton Dr	30	B4
Hilton Pl	30	C4
Hilton Rd	30	A4
Hilton St	30	B5
Hilton Ter	30	B4
Hilton Wk	30	B4
Holburn Pl	32	D5
Holburn Rd	32	C4
Holburn St	32	D5
Holland Pl	30	D6
Holland St	30	D6
Hollybank Pl	32	D4
Hosefield Av	32	B1
Hosefield Rd	32	B1
Howburn Pl	32	D4
Hunter Pl	31	F6
Huntly St	32	D2
Hutcheon Ct	32	D1
Hutcheon Gdns	31	F1
Hutcheon St	32	D1
Hutchison Ter	32	A6

I

Street	Page	Grid
Inverdon Ct	31	F2
Irvine Pl	32	C5

J

Street	Page	Grid
Jacks Brae	32	D2
Jamaica St	30	D6
James St	33	G2

Name	Ref		Name	Ref
Jamiesons Quay	33 F3		Merkland Rd	31 F5
Jasmine Pl	33 F1		Merkland Rd E	31 F5
Jasmine Ter	33 F1		Meston Wk	31 E4
Jasmine Way	33 F1		Midchingle Rd	33 G3
Johns Pk Pl	30 B1		Middlefield Cres	30 A3
John St	33 E1		Middlefield Ter	30 A3
Jopps La	33 E1		Mile-End Av	32 B1
Jubilee Gait	32 C6		Mile-End La	32 B1
Justice Mill La	32 D3		Mile-End Pl	32 B1
Jute St	31 E6		Millbank La	30 D6
			Millbank Pl	30 D6
K			Millburn St	33 E4
Kerloch Gdns	33 F5		Mill Ct	30 A2
Kerloch Pl	33 F6		Miller St	33 G2
Kettocks Mill Rd	31 E2		Montgomery Cres	30 C2
Kidd St	32 D2		Montgomery Rd	30 C2
King George VI Br	33 E6		Morgan Rd	30 A5
Kings Cres	31 F6		Morningfield Ms	32 A2
King's Gate	32 A2		Morningside Gdns	32 A6
Kingsland Pl	33 E1		Morningside La	32 A6
King St	31 F5		Morningside Pl	32 A6
King St (Woodside)	30 B3		Morningside Rd	32 A6
Kinnaird Pl	30 D2		Morningside Ter	32 A6
Kinord Circle	31 E1		Morven Pl	33 G5
Kintore Pl	32 D1		Mosman Gdns	30 A4
Kirkhill Pl	33 H6		Mosman Pl	30 A4
Kirkhill Rd	33 G6		Mounthooly	31 F6
Kittybrewster Sq	30 C5		Mounthooly Way	31 F6
			Mount Pleasant	31 G1
L			Mount St	32 D1
Laburnum Wk	30 A5		Murray Ct	30 A2
Ladywell Pl	33 H5		Murray Ter	33 E5
Lamond Pl	30 D6			
Langstane Pl	33 E3		**N**	
Laurel Av	30 B1		Nellfield Pl	32 C4
Laurel Braes	30 B1		Nelson Ct	31 F6
Laurel Dr	30 A1		Nelson La	31 F6
Laurel Gdns	30 B1		Nelson St	31 F6
Laurel Gro	30 B1		Newlands Av	32 B6
Laurel Pl	30 A1		Newlands Cres	32 B6
Laurel Rd	30 A1		Norfolk Rd	32 B5
Laurel Ter	30 B1		North Esplanade E	33 G3
Laurel Vw	30 A1		North Esplanade W	33 F4
Laurelwood Av	30 C5		Northfield Pl	32 D2
Laurel Wynd	30 B1		North Grampian Circle	33 G5
Leadside Rd	32 D2		Northsea Ct	31 G3
Learney Pl	32 A4		Novar Pl	32 D1
Lemon St	33 G1			
Leslie Rd	30 C4		**O**	
Leslie Ter	30 D5		Oakhill Cres	32 A2
Lilybank Pl	30 C4		Oakhill Rd	32 A2
Lillie St	33 H2		Old Ch Rd	33 G6
Linksfield Ct	31 G4		Old Ford Rd	33 F4
Linksfield Gdns	31 F5		Orchard Pl	31 E5
Linksfield Pl	31 F5		Orchard Rd	31 F5
Linksfield Rd	31 F5		Orchard St	31 E5
Links Pl	33 H2		Orchard Wk	31 E5
Links Rd	33 H1		Osborne Pl	32 B2
Links Rd (Bridge of Don)	31 G1		Oscar Pl	33 G5
Links St	33 H2		Oscar Rd	33 G5
Links Vw	31 G5			
Livingstone Ct	31 F3		**P**	
Loanhead Pl	32 C1		Palmerston Pl	33 F4
Loanhead Ter	32 C1		Palmerston Rd	33 F4
Loanhead Wk	32 C1		Park Rd	31 G6
Loch St	33 E1		Park St	33 G1
Loirston Pl	33 H5		Pennan Rd	30 D2
Lord Hay's Ct	31 G2		Picktillum Av	30 C5
Lord Hay's Gro	31 F2		Picktillum Pl	30 C5
Louisville Av	32 A4		Pirie's Ct	30 C4
			Pirie's La	30 C4
M			Pitstruan Pl	32 C4
Maberly St	33 E1		Pitstruan Ter	32 C5
Mackie Pl	32 D2		Pittodrie La	31 F5
Mansefield Pl	33 H5		Pittodrie Pl	31 F5
Mansefield Rd	33 H4		Pittodrie St	31 F5
Margaret Pl	32 C6		Polmuir Av	33 E5
Marine Ter	33 E4		Polmuir Pl	33 E5
Marischal St	33 F2		Polmuir Rd	33 E4
Market St	33 F2		Polwarth Rd	33 F5
Marquis Rd	30 C3		Portal Cres	30 D3
Matthews Quay	33 H3		Portal Ter	30 D4
Mayfield Gdns	32 A4		Portland St	33 E3
Meadow La	30 D2		Powis Circle	30 D4
Meadow Pl	30 C2		Powis Cres	30 D4
Mearns Quay	33 H3		Powis La	31 E6
Mearns St	33 G2		Powis Pl	30 D6
Menzies Rd	33 G4		Powis Ter	30 D5
Merkland La	31 G5			
Merkland Pl	31 F5			

Name	Ref		Name	Ref
Poynernook Rd	33 F3		St. Peter's Pl	31 F5
Primrosehill Dr	30 C4		St. Peter St	31 F6
Primrosehill Gdns	30 C4		St. Swithin Row	32 B3
Primrosehill Pl	30 C4		St. Swithin St	32 B3
Prince Arthur St	32 C2		Salisbury Ct	32 C5
Princes St	33 F1		Salisbury Pl	32 C5
Printfield Ter	30 C3		Salisbury Ter	32 B5
Printfield Wk	30 C3		Sandilands Dr	30 C3
Promenade Ct	31 G4		School Av	31 F4
Prospect Ct	33 F4		School Dr	31 F4
Prospect Ter	33 F4		Schoolhill	33 E2
			School Rd	31 F4
Q			School Ter	31 F4
Queen Elizabeth II Br	33 F4		Scotstown Gdns	31 F1
Queens Ct	32 A4		Seaforth Rd	31 F6
Queen's Cross	32 B3		Seamount Rd	33 F1
Queens Gdns	32 B3		Seaton Av	31 F3
Queen's Gate	32 A3		Seaton Cres	31 G3
Queens La N	32 B3		Seaton Dr	31 F3
Queens La S	32 A3		Seaton Gdns	31 F3
Queens Links Leisure Pk	33 H1		Seaton Ho	31 G3
Queens Ter	32 C3		Seaton Pl	31 F3
Queen St	33 F2		Seaton Pl E	31 F3
Queen St (Woodside)	30 B3		Seaton Rd	31 F4
			Seaton Wk	31 F3
R			Seaview Ho	31 G4
Raeburn Pl	33 E1		Seaview Rd	31 F1
Raeden Av	32 A1		Shiprow	33 F2
Raeden Pk Rd	32 A1		Short Loanings	32 D1
Raik Rd	33 F3		Simpson Rd	31 F1
Rattray Pl	30 D2		Sinclair Pl	33 H4
Regent Ct	31 G4		Sinclair Rd	33 G4
Regent Quay	33 G2		Skene La	32 D2
Regent Rd	33 G3		Skene Sq	32 D1
Regent Wk	31 F4		Skene St	32 D2
Richmondhill Ct	32 A2		Skene Ter	33 E2
Richmondhill Gdns	32 A1		Smithfield La	30 A3
Richmondhill Pl	32 A1		Smithfield Rd	30 B3
Richmondhill Rd	32 A1		Society La	30 B3
Richmond St	32 D1		South Anderson Dr	32 B6
Richmond Ter	32 D1		South Coll St	33 F3
Richmond Wk	32 D1		South Crown St	33 E4
Ritchie Pl	30 C2		South Esplanade E	33 G4
Riverside Dr	32 D6		South Esplanade W	33 F4
Riverside Ter	32 C6		South Grampian Circle	33 G5
Rockall Pl	33 H5		South Mile End	32 D5
Rockall Rd	33 H5		South Mt St	32 D1
Rodger's Wk	33 E1		Spademill La	32 A3
Rosebank Pl	32 D4		Spademill Rd	32 A3
Rosebank Ter	33 E4		Spa St	33 E1
Rosebery St	32 B1		Spital	31 E5
Rosehill Av	30 A4		Spital Wk	31 E5
Rosehill Ct	30 A5		Springbank St	33 E3
Rosehill Cres	30 B4		Springbank Ter	33 E3
Rosehill Dr	30 A4		Spring Gdn	33 E1
Rosehill Pl	30 B4		Stafford St	30 D6
Rosehill Ter	30 B4		Stanley St	32 C3
Rosemount Pl	32 C1		Station Rd	30 B2
Rosemount Viaduct	32 D2		Stell Rd	33 F3
Rose St	32 D2		Stewart Pk Ct	30 A4
Roslin Pl	33 G1		Stewart Pk Pl	30 A4
Roslin St	31 G6		Summerfield Ter	33 F1
Roslin Ter	31 F6		Summer St	32 D2
Rowan Rd	30 A5		Summer St (Woodside)	30 B3
Rubislaw Pl	32 D3		Sunnybank Pl	31 E5
Rubislaw Ter	32 C3		Sunnybank Rd	31 E5
Rubislaw Ter La	32 C3		Sunnyside Av	31 E5
Russell Rd	33 F4		Sunnyside Gdns	31 E5
Ruthrie Ct	32 B6		Sunnyside Rd	30 D5
Ruthrieston Circle	32 C6		Sunnyside Ter	31 E5
Ruthrieston Cres	32 C6		Sycamore Pl	33 E5
Ruthrieston Pl	32 C6			
Ruthrieston Rd	32 B6		**T**	
			Tanfield Av	30 C3
S			Tanfield Wk	30 C3
St. Andrew St	33 E1		Tarbothill Rd	30 D1
St. Clair St	33 F1		Tedder Rd	30 D3
St. Clement St	33 G2		Tedder St	30 D3
St. Machar Dr	30 D4		Thistle Ct	32 D2
St. Machar Ind Est	30 D3		Thistle La	32 D2
St. Machar Pl	31 F3		Thistle Pl	32 D3
St. Machar Rd	30 D3		Thistle St	32 D3
St. Nicholas Cen	33 F2		Thomas Glover Pl	31 E1
St. Ninians Pl	31 F3		Thomson St	32 C1
St. Ninians Pl	31 F2		Thorngrove Av	32 A5
St. Peter La	31 F6		Thorngrove Ct	32 A5
St. Peter's Gate	31 F5		Thorngrove Cres	32 A5

Name	Ref
Thorngrove Pl	32 A5
Tillydrone Av	31 E3
Tillydrone Ct	30 D2
Tillydrone Rd	31 E3
Tillydrone Ter	30 D3
Trinity Quay	33 F2
Tullos Circle	33 G5
Tullos Cres	33 H5
Tullos Pl	33 H5
U	
Union Glen	32 D3
Union Gro	32 C3
Union Gro La	32 C4
Union Row	32 D3
Union St	32 D3
Union Ter	33 E2
Union Wynd	32 D2
University Rd	31 E4
Upperkirkgate	33 F2
Urquhart La	31 F6
Urquhart Pl	31 G6
Urquhart Rd	31 F6
Urquhart St	31 G6
Urquhart Ter	31 G6
V	
Victoria Br	33 G3
Victoria Rd	33 G4
Victoria St	32 D2
View Ter	32 D1
Virginia St	33 F2
W	
Wales St	33 G1
Walker La	33 G4
Walker Pl	33 G4
Walker Rd	33 F5
Wallfield Cres	32 C2
Wallfield Pl	32 C2
Wapping St	33 E2
Waterloo Quay	33 G2
Watson La	32 C1
Watson St	32 C1
Wavell Cres	30 C2
Waverley La	32 D2
Waverley Pl	32 D3
Wellington Brae	33 F4
Wellington Br	33 F5
Wellington Pl	33 E3
Wellington Rd	33 F5
Wellington St	33 H2
Westburn Cres	30 B6
Westburn Dr	30 B6
Westburn Pk	30 C6
Westburn Rd	32 C1
Western Rd	30 C3
Westfield Rd	32 C2
Westfield Ter	32 C2
West Mt St	32 D1
West N St	33 F1
Whinhill Gdns	33 E5
Whinhill Gate	33 E4
Whinhill Rd	32 D5
Whitehall Pl	32 C2
Whitehall Rd	32 B2
Whitehall Ter	32 C2
Willowbank Rd	32 D4
Willowdale Pl	33 F1
Wingate Pl	30 D3
Wingate Rd	30 D3
Woolmanhill	33 E2
Y	
York Pl	33 H2
York St	33 H2

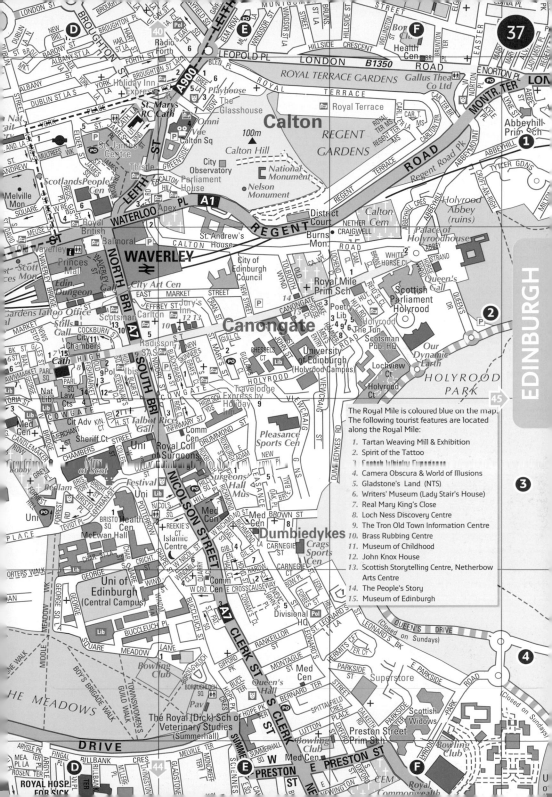

EDINBURGH

Calton

REGENT GARDENS

Royal Terrace Gardens

Gallus Thea Co Ltd

Royal Terrace

Holyrood Abbey (ruins)

Palace of Holyroodhouse

HOLYROOD PARK

Canongate

Scottish Parliament Holyrood

Our Dynamic Earth

University of Edinburgh (Holyrood Campus)

WAVERLEY

Dumbiedykes

Uni of Edinburgh (Central Campus)

THE MEADOWS

DRIVE

Queen's Drive (Closed on Sundays)

The Royal Mile is coloured blue on the map.
The following tourist features are located
along the Royal Mile:

1. Tartan Weaving Mill & Exhibition
2. Spirit of the Tattoo
3. Scotch Whisky Experience
4. Camera Obscura & World of Illusions
5. Gladstone's Land (NTS)
6. Writers' Museum (Lady Stair's House)
7. Real Mary King's Close
8. Loch Ness Discovery Centre
9. The Tron Old Town Information Centre
10. Brass Rubbing Centre
11. Museum of Childhood
12. John Knox House
13. Scottish Storytelling Centre, Netherbow Arts Centre
14. The People's Story
15. Museum of Edinburgh

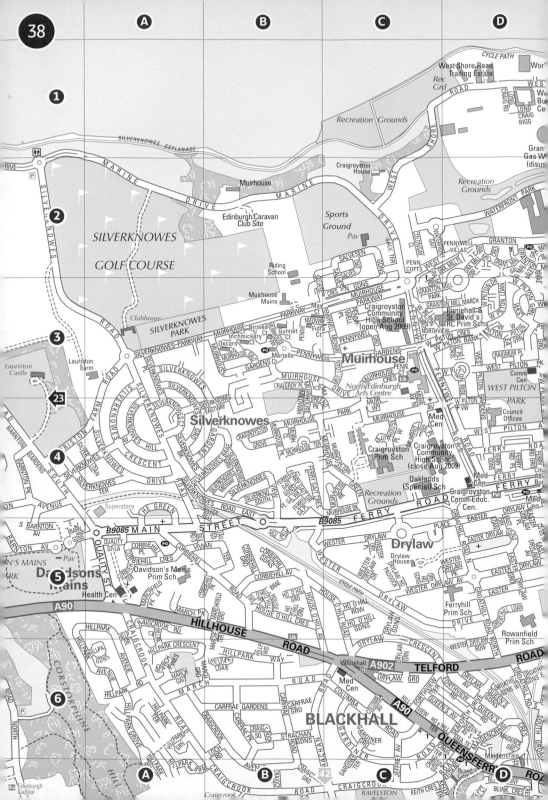

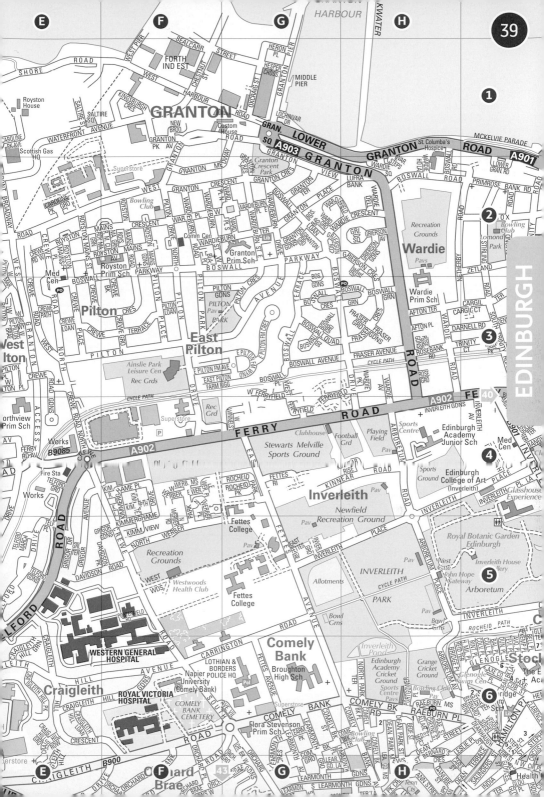

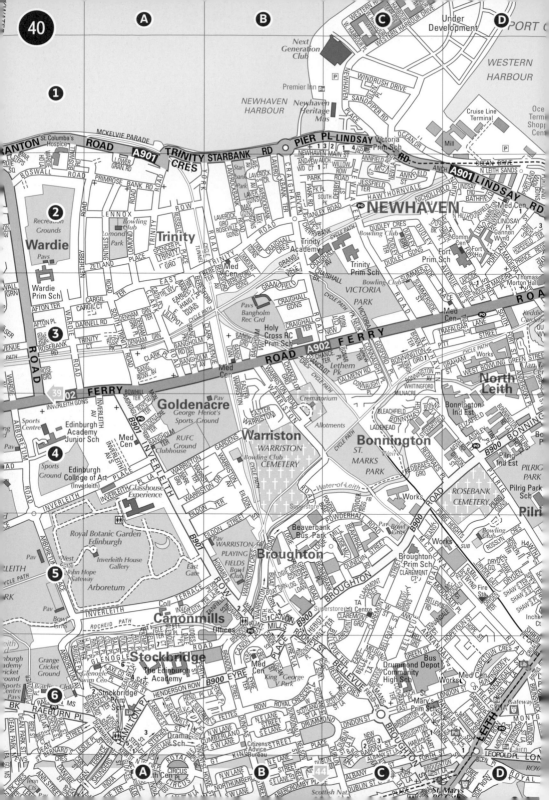

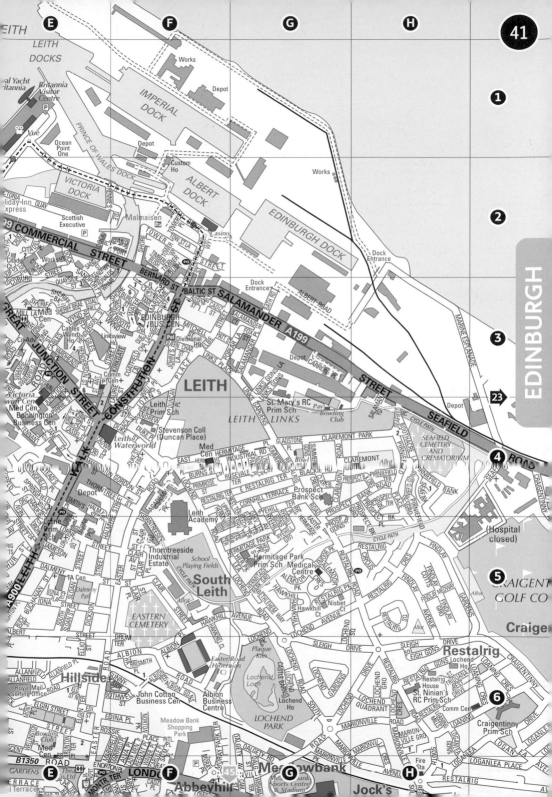

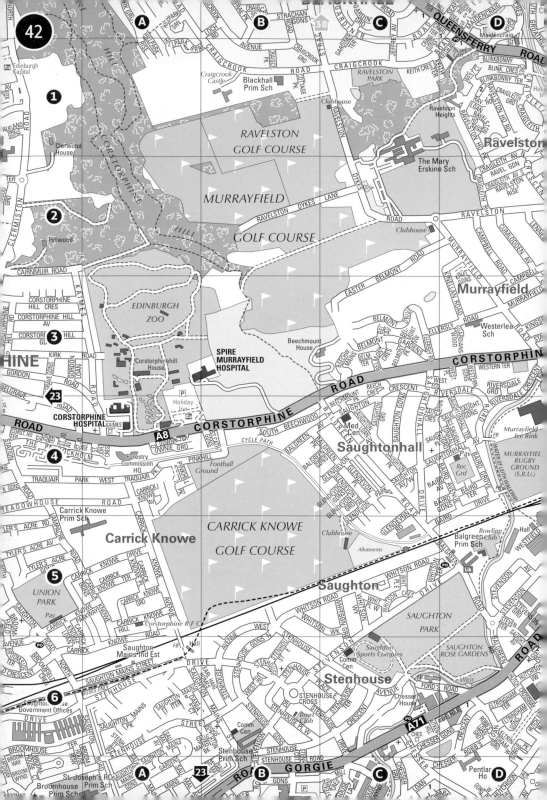

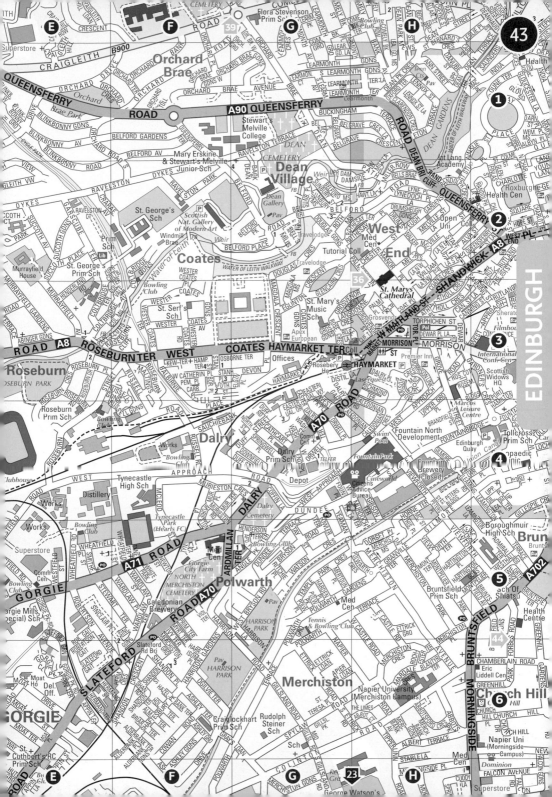

EDINBURGH

There are street names in this index which are followed by a number in **bold**. These numbers can be found on the map where there is insufficient space to show the street name in full.

A

Abbeyhill	37	F1
Abbeyhill Cres	37	F2
Abbeyhill Ind Est	45	F1
Abbey La	45	F1
Abbeymount	37	F1
Abbey Strand	37	F2
Abbey St	45	F1
Abbotsford Ct	43	H6
Abbotsford Cres	43	H6
Abbotsford Pk	43	H6
Abercorn Cres	45	H2
Abercorn Dr	45	H2
Abercorn Gro	45	H2
Abercorn Rd	45	H2
Abercromby Pl	36	C1
Abinger Gdns	43	E3
Academy Pk	41	F4
Academy St	41	F4
Admiral Ter	44	A5
Admiralty St	41	E2
Advocates Cl **1**	37	D2
Afton Pl	39	H3
Afton Ter	39	H3
Agnew Ter	40	C3
Ainslie Pl	36	A1
Aird's Cl	36	C3
Aitkenhill	42	C6
Albany La	37	D1
Albany St	37	D1
Albany St La	37	D1
Albert Dock	41	F2
Albert Pl	40	D6
Albert Rd	41	G3
Albert St	41	E5
Albert Ter	43	H6
Albion Business Cen	41	F6
Albion Gdns	41	F6
Albion Pl	41	F6
Albion Rd	41	F6
Albion Ter	41	F6
Albyn Pl	36	B1
Alderbank Pl	43	F6
Alderbank Ter	43	F6
Alemoor Cres	41	G5
Alemoor Pk	41	G5
Alexander Dr	43	E5
Alfred Pl	45	E5
Allanfield	41	E6
Allanfield Pl	41	E6
Allan St	39	H6
Almondbank Ter	43	F6
Alvanley Ter **1**	44	A5
Alva Pl	45	F1
Alva St	36	A2
Anchor Cl **11**	37	D2
Anchorfield	40	C2
Anderson Pl	40	D3
Andrew Wd Ct	40	B2
Angle Pk Ter	43	G5
Annandale St	41	E6
Annandale St La	40	D6
Annfield	40	C2
Annfield St	40	C2
Ann St	36	A1
Ann Ter	45	F1
Antigua St **1**	40	D6
Appin Ter	43	E6
Arboretum Av	39	H6
Arboretum Pl	39	H5
Arboretum Rd	39	H4
Archibald Pl	36	C3
Arden St	44	B5
Ardmillan Pl	43	G5
Ardmillan Ter	43	G5
Ardmillan Ter La **1**	43	G5
Argyle Pk Ter	44	C5
Argyle Pl	44	C5
Argyle St	40	D2
Argyll Ter **2**	36	A3
Arthur St	41	E5
Arthur St La	41	E5

Ashley Gro	43	F6
Ashley Pl	40	D4
Ashley Ter	43	F6
Ashville Ter	41	G5
Assembly St	41	F3
Atholl Cres	36	A3
Atholl Cres La	36	A3
Atholl Pl	36	A3
Atholl Ter **3**	36	A3
Auchinleck Ct	40	B2
Auchinleck's Brae **1**	40	B2
Avenue Vil	39	G6
Avondale Pl	40	A6

B

Back Dean	43	G2
Baird Av	42	D4
Baird Dr	42	C5
Baird Gdns	42	C4
Baird Gro	42	D4
Baird Ter	42	D4
Bakehouse Cl	37	E2
Baker's Pl **1**	40	A6
Balbirnie Pl	43	F3
Balfour Pl	40	D5
Balfour St	41	E4
Balgreen Av	42	B4
Balgreen Gdns	42	B4
Balgreen Pk	42	B4
Balgreen Rd	42	C4
Ballantyne La **1**	41	E3
Ballantyne Rd	41	E3
Balmoral Pl	40	A6
Baltic St	41	F3
Bangholm Av	40	A3
Bangholm Bower Av	40	A3
Bangholm Gro	40	B3
Bangholm Ln	40	B3
Bangholm Pk	40	A3
Bangholm Pl	40	A3
Bangholm Rd	40	A3
Bangholm Ter	40	A4
Bangholm Vw	40	B3
Bangor Rd	40	D3
Bank St	37	D2
Barclay Pl	36	B4
Barclay Ter	44	A5
Baronscourt Rd	45	H1
Barony Pl **3**	40	C6
Barony St	40	C6
Barrie's Cl **14**	37	D2
Bathfield	40	D2
Bath Rd	41	G3
Baxter's Pl **1**	37	E1
Beaufort Rd	44	C6
Beaverbank Business Pk	40	B5
Beaverbank Pl	40	B5
Beaverhall Rd	40	C5
Bedford Ct	39	H6
Bedford St	39	H6
Beechmount Cres	42	C3
Beechmount Pk	42	C4
Beechwood Mains	42	C3
Beechwood Ter	41	G5
Belford Av	43	F1
Belford Br	43	G2
Belford Gdns	43	F1
Belford Ms	43	G2
Belford Pk	43	G2
Belford Pl	43	F2
Belford Rd	43	G2
Belford Ter **1**	43	G2
Belgrave Cres	43	G1
Belgrave Cres La	43	G1
Belgrave Ms	43	G1
Belgrave Pl	43	G1
Bellevue	40	C6
Bellevue Cres	40	C6
Bellevue Gdns	40	C5
Bellevue Gro	40	C6
Bellevue La	40	C6

Bellevue Pl	40	C6
Bellevue Rd	40	C6
Bellevue St	40	C6
Bellevue Ter	40	C5
Bell Pl	40	A6
Bells Brae	36	A2
Bell's Mills	43	G2
Bell's Wynd **2**	37	D2
Belmont Av	42	C3
Belmont Cres	42	C3
Belmont Dr	42	C3
Belmont Gdns	42	C3
Belmont Pk	42	C3
Belmont Ter	42	C3
Belmont Vw	42	C3
Belvedere Pk	40	B2
Beresford Av	40	B2
Beresford Gdns	40	A3
Beresford Pl	40	A3
Beresford Ter	40	A3
Bernard St	41	F2
Bernard Ter	37	E4
Bethlehem Way	41	G5
Birnies Ct	38	B3
Blackadder Pl	39	F2
Blacket Av	45	E5
Blacket Pl	45	E5
Blackford Rd	44	B6
Blackfriars St	37	E2
Blackie Rd	41	G4
Blackwood Cres	44	D5
Blair St	37	D2
Blandfield	40	C5
Blantyre Ter	43	H6
Bleachfield	40	C4
Blenheim Pl	37	E1
Blinkbonny Av	43	E1
Blinkbonny Cres	42	D1
Blinkbonny Gdns	43	E1
Blinkbonny Gro	43	E1
Blinkbonny Gro W	43	E1
Blinkbonny Rd	43	E1
Blinkbonny Ter	42	D1
Boat Grn	40	B5
Bonar Pl	40	C3
Bonnington Av	40	C3
Bonnington Business Cen	41	E4
Bonnington Gait **1**	40	D4
Bonnington Gro	40	C3
Bonnington Ind Est	40	D4
Bonnington Rd	40	D4
Bonnington Rd La	40	D4
Bonnington Ter	40	C3
Bonnyhaugh	40	C4
Bonnyhaugh La	40	C4
Boothacre Cotts **2**	41	H4
Boothacre La	41	H4
Boroughloch	37	E4
Boroughloch Sq	37	E4
Borthwick Pl	43	F3
Borthwick's Cl **3**	37	D2
Boswall Av	39	G3
Boswall Cres	39	G3
Boswall Dr	39	G2
Boswall Gdns	39	G3
Boswall Grn	39	H3
Boswall Gro	39	G3
Boswall Ln	39	G2
Boswall Ms	39	G2
Boswall Parkway	39	F2
Boswall Pl	39	G3
Boswall Quad	39	G3
Boswall Rd	39	H2
Boswall Sq	39	G3
Boswall Ter	39	G3
Bothwell St	41	E6
Bowhill Ter	40	A4
Bowie's Cl **1**	41	E3
Bowling Grn, The	41	E3
Bowling La **8**	41	E3
Bowmont Pl	37	E4
Boyd's Entry **2**	37	E2

Boy's Brigade Wk	37	D4
Brandfield St	36	A4
Brandon St	40	B6
Brandon Ter	40	B6
Breadalbane St	40	D3
Breadalbane Ter **5**	36	A3
Bread St	36	B3
Bread St La	36	B3
Brewery La **2**	41	E3
Briarbank Ter	43	F6
Bridge Pl	39	H6
Briery Bauks	37	E3
Brighton St	37	D3
Bright's Cres	45	E6
Bright Ter **8**	36	A3
Bristo Pl	37	D3
Bristo Port	37	D3
Bristo Sq	37	D3
Broad Wynd **7**	41	F3
Broomhouse Row	42	A6
Brougham Pl	36	C4
Brougham St	36	B4
Broughton Mkt	40	C6
Broughton Pl	40	C6
Broughton Pl La	40	C6
Broughton Rd	40	C5
Broughton St	40	C6
Broughton St La	37	D1
Brown's Cl	37	F2
Brown's Pl **4**	36	C3
Brown St	37	E3
Brown St La **8**	37	E3
Brunswick Pl	40	D6
Brunswick Rd	40	D6
Brunswick St	40	D6
Brunswick Ter **1**	41	E6
Brunton Gdns **2**	41	E6
Brunton Pl	41	E6
Brunton Ter	41	E6
Bruntsfield Av	44	A5
Bruntsfield Cres	44	A5
Bruntsfield Gdns	44	A6
Bruntsfield Pl	43	H6
Bruntsfield Ter	44	A5
Bryson Rd	43	G5
Buccleuch Pl	37	D4
Buccleuch St	37	E4
Buccleuch Ter	37	E4
Buchanan St	41	E5
Buckingham Ter	43	G1
Bull's Cl **5**	37	F2
Burgess St	41	F3
Burgess Ter	45	F6
Burlington St	40	D3
Burns St	41	F4

C

Cables Wynd	41	E3
Cables Wynd Ho	41	E3
Cadiz St	41	F3
Cadzow Pl	45	F1
Caithness Pl	40	A3
Caledonian Cres	36	A4
Caledonian Pl	43	G4
Caledonian Rd	36	A3
Calton Hill	37	E1
Calton Rd	37	E2
Calton Sq	37	E1
Cambridge Av	40	D5
Cambridge Gdns	40	D5
Cambridge St	36	B3
Cambridge St La **3**	36	B3
Cambusnethan St	45	G1
Cameron Ho Av	45	G6
Campbell Av	42	C3
Campbell Rd	42	D2
Campbell's Cl	37	F2
Candlemaker Row	37	D3
Canning St	36	A3
Canning St La	36	A3
Cannon Wynd	40	D2

Canon Ct **3**	40	B5
Canongate	37	E2
Canon La	40	B6
Canonmills	40	B5
Canonmills Br **2**	40	B5
Canon St	40	B6
Carberry Pl	43	F3
Carfrae Gdns	38	B6
Carfrae Gro	38	B6
Carfrae Pk	38	B6
Carfrae Rd	38	B6
Cargil Ct	39	H3
Cargil Ter	40	A3
Carlton St	36	A1
Carlton Ter	37	F1
Carlton Ter Brae	37	F1
Carlton Ter La	37	F1
Carlton Ter Ms	37	F1
Carlton Wynd	37	E2
Carlyle Pl	45	F1
Carnegie Ct	37	E3
Carnegie St	37	E3
Caroline Pk Av	39	E1
Caroline Pk Gro	39	E2
Carpet La	41	F3
Carrick Knowe Av	42	A4
Carrick Knowe Gdns	42	A5
Carrick Knowe Gro	42	A5
Carrick Knowe Hill	42	A5
Carrick Knowe Pl	42	A5
Carrick Knowe Ter	42	A5
Carrington Rd	39	F6
Carron Pl	41	G3
Carrubber's Cl **5**	37	D2
Casselbank St	41	E4
Cassel's La	41	E4
Castlehill	36	C2
Castle St	36	B2
Castle Ter	36	B3
Castle Wynd N **11**	36	C3
Castle Wynd S **6**	36	C3
Cathcart Pl	43	G4
Cathedral La	37	D1
Catherine Pl	40	B3
Causeway, The	45	H4
Causewayside	44	D5
Chalmers Bldgs **2**	36	B4
Chalmers Cl **4**	37	E2
Chalmers Cres	44	C5
Chalmers St	36	C3
Chamberlain Rd	44	A6
Chambers St	37	D3
Chancelot Cres	40	B3
Chancelot Gro	40	B3
Chancelot Ter	40	B3
Chapel La **2**	41	F3
Chapel St	37	E3
Chapel Wynd **7**	36	C3
Charlesfield **1**	37	D3
Charles St	37	D3
Charles St La	37	D3
Charlotte La	36	B2
Charlotte Sq	36	B2
Chessels Ct	37	E2
Chesser Av	42	C6
Chesser Cotts **1**	42	D6
Chesser Ct	42	C6
Chesser Gdns	42	C6
Chester St	36	A2
Chestnut St	39	F1
Cheyne St	39	H6
Chuckie Pend	36	B3
Church Hill	44	A6
Church Hill Dr	44	A6
Church Hill Pl	44	A6
Circus Gdns	36	B1
Circus La	40	A6
Circus Pl	36	B1
Citadel Ct	41	E2
Citadel Pl	41	E2
Citadel St **2**	41	E2
Clarebank Cres	41	G4
Claremont Bk	40	C6

Name	Ref
Claremont Ct	40 C5
Claremont Cres	40 C5
Claremont Gdns	41 G4
Claremont Gro	40 C5
Claremont Pk	41 G4
Claremont Rd	41 G4
Clarence St	40 A6
Clarendon Cres	36 A1
Clark Av	40 B3
Clark Pl	40 A3
Clark Rd	40 A3
Clearburn Cres	45 G6
Clearburn Gdns	45 G6
Clearburn Rd	45 G6
Clerk St	37 E4
Clifton Ter	36 A3
Clinton Rd	44 A6
Clockmill La	45 G1
Coalhill	41 E3
Coates Cres	36 A3
Coates Gdns	43 G3
Coates Pl	36 A3
Coatfield La	41 F3
Cobden Cres	45 E6
Cobden Rd	45 E6
Cobden Ter 7	36 A3
Coburg St	41 E3
Cochrane Pl 1	41 F4
Cochran Pl	40 C6
Cochran Ter	40 C6
Cockburn St	37 D2
Coffin La	43 G4
Coinyie Ho Cl 1	37 E2
College Wynd 2	37 D3
Collins Pl	40 A6
Colonsay Cl	38 C2
Coltbridge Av	43 E3
Coltbridge Gdns	43 F3
Coltbridge Millside	43 E3
Coltbridge Ter	43 E3
Coltbridge Vale	43 F3
Columba Av	38 C6
Columba Rd	38 C6
Colville Pl	40 A6
Comely Bk	39 G6
Comely Bk Av	39 H6
Comely Bk Gro	43 G1
Comely Bk Pl	39 H6
Comely Bk Pl Ms 2	39 H6
Comely Bk Rd	39 H6
Comely Bk Row	39 H6
Comely Bk St	39 G6
Comely Bk Ter	39 G6
Comely Grn Cres	45 F1
Comely Grn Pl	45 F1
Commercial St	41 E2
Commercial Wf 1	41 F2
Conference Sq	36 B3
Connaught Pl	40 C3
Considine Gdns	45 H1
Considine Ter	45 H1
Constitution St	41 E4
Convening Ct 1	36 A2
Cooper's Cl 3	37 F2
Corbiehill Av	38 B5
Corbiehill Cres	38 A5
Corbiehill Gdns	38 B5
Corbiehill Gro	38 B5
Corbiehill Pk	38 A5
Corbiehill Pl	38 A5
Corbiehill Rd	38 A5
Corbiehill Ter	38 A5
Cornhill Ter	41 G4
Cornwallis Pl	40 B6
Cornwall St	36 B3
Coronation Wk	36 C4
Corstorphine Rd	42 D3
Corunna Pl	41 E3
Cottage Pk	38 B5
Couper Fld	41 E2
Couper St	41 E2
Cowan Rd	43 F6
Cowan's Cl	37 E4
Cowgate	37 D3
Cowgatehead	37 D3
Coxfield	42 D6
Coxfield La 2	42 D6
Craigcrook Av	38 B6
Craigcrook Gdns	42 C1
Craigcrook Gro	38 B6
Craigcrook Pk	42 B1
Craigcrook Pl 1	38 D6
Craigcrook Rd	42 C1
Craigcrook Sq	38 B6
Craigcrook Ter	38 C6
Craighall Av	40 B2
Craighall Bk	40 B2
Craighall Cres	40 B2
Craighall Gdns	40 B3
Craighall Rd	40 B2
Craighall Ter	40 B3
Craigleith Av N	42 D2
Craigleith Av S	42 D2
Craigleith Bk	42 D1
Craigleith Cres	42 D1
Craigleith Dr	42 D1
Craigleith Gdns	42 D1
Craigleith Gro	42 D1
Craigleith Hill	43 E1
Craigleith Hill Av	38 D6
Craigleith Hill Cres	39 E6
Craigleith Hill Gdns	39 E6
Craigleith Hill Grn	39 E6
Craigleith Hill Gro	39 E6
Craigleith Hill Ln	39 E6
Craigleith Hill Pk	39 E6
Craigleith Hill Row	39 E6
Craigleith Ri	42 D2
Craigleith Rd	43 E1
Craigleith Vw	42 D2
Craigmuir Pl	38 D3
Craigroyston Gro	38 B4
Craigroyston Pl	38 B3
Cranston St	37 E2
Crarae Av	42 D2
Crawford Br 1	41 F6
Crewe Bk	39 F3
Crewe Cres	39 E3
Crewe Gro	39 F3
Crewe Ln	39 E3
Crewe Path	39 E3
Crewe Pl	39 E3
Crewe Rd Gdns	39 E3
Crewe Rd N	39 E3
Crewe Rd S	39 F3
Crewe Rd W	39 E3
Crewe Ter	39 E3
Crewe Toll	39 E3
Crichton's Cl 4	37 F2
Crichton St	37 D3
Crighton Pl	41 E5
Croall Pl	40 D6
Croft-an-righ	37 F1
Cromwell Pl	41 E2
Crown Pl	41 E4
Crown St	41 E4
Cumberland St	40 B6
Cumberland St N E La	40 B6
Cumberland St N W La	40 B6
Cumberland St S E La	40 B6
Cumberland St S W La	40 B6
Cumin Pl	44 D5
Cumlodden Av	42 D2
Cunningham Pl 1	41 E4

D

Name	Ref
Daisy Ter 3	43 F6
Dalgety Av	41 G6
Dalgety Rd	41 G6
Dalgety St	45 G1
Dalkeith Rd	37 F4
Dalkeith Rd Ms	45 F6
Dalmeny Rd	40 C3
Dalmeny St	41 E5
Dalry Gait	43 G3
Dalrymple Cres	44 D6
Dalry Pl	36 A3
Dalry Rd	43 G4
Dalziel Pl 1	45 F1
Damside	43 G2
Dania Ct	42 A6
Danube St	36 A1
Darnaway St	36 B1
Darnell Rd	39 H3
Davidson Gdns	38 B5
Davidson Pk	39 E5
Davidson Rd	39 E5
Davie St	37 E3
Dean Bk La	40 A6
Dean Br	36 A1
Deanery Cl 1	45 H1
Deanhaugh St	40 A6
Dean Pk Cres	36 A1
Dean Pk Ms	39 H6
Dean Pk St	39 H6
Dean Path	43 G1
Dean Path Bldgs 2	36 A2
Dean St	39 H6
Dean Ter	36 A1
Delhaig	42 D6
Denham Grn Av	40 A3
Denham Grn Pl	40 A3
Denham Grn Ter	40 A3
Derby St	40 C2
Devon Pl	43 G3
Dewar Pl	36 A3
Dewar Pl La	36 A3
Dick Pl	44 C6
Dicksonfield	40 D6
Dickson's Cl 5	37 E2
Dickson St	41 E5
Distillery La	43 G3
Dock Pl	41 E2
Dock St	41 E2
Dorset Pl	43 H5
Douglas Cres	43 G2
Douglas Gdns	43 G2
Douglas Gdns Ms 3	43 G2
Douglas Ter 1	36 A3
Doune Ter	36 B1
Downfield Pl	43 G4
Downie Gro	42 A4
Downie Ter	42 A4
Drumdryan St	36 B3
Drummond Pl	40 B6
Drummond St	37 E3
Drumsheugh Gdns	36 A2
Drumsheugh Pl 3	36 A2
Drum Ter	41 F6
Dryden Gait	40 D5
Dryden Gdns	40 D5
Dryden Pl	45 E5
Dryden St	40 D5
Dryden Ter	40 D5
Drylaw Av	38 D6
Drylaw Cres	38 C5
Drylaw Gdns	38 C5
Drylaw Grn	38 C6
Drylaw Gro	38 C6
Drylaw Ho Gdns	38 C5
Drylaw Ho Paddock	38 C5
Dublin Meuse	36 C1
Dublin St	40 C6
Dublin St La N	40 C6
Dublin St La S	37 D1
Dudley Av	40 C2
Dudley Av S	40 D3
Dudley Bk	40 C2
Dudley Cres	40 C2
Dudley Gdns	40 C2
Dudley Gro	40 C2
Dudley Ter	40 C2
Duff Rd	43 G4
Duff St	43 G4
Duff St La	43 G4
Duke Pl	41 F4
Duke St	41 F4
Duke St Glebe	41 F4
Duke's Wk	45 G2
Dumbiedykes Rd	37 F3
Dunbar St	36 B3
Duncan Pl	41 F4
Duncan St	44 D6
Dundas St	40 B6
Dundee St	43 G4
Dundee Ter	43 G5
Dundonald St	40 B6
Dunedin St	40 C5
Dunlop's Ct 12	36 C3
Dunrobin Pl	40 A6

E

Name	Ref
Earl Grey St	36 B3
Earl Haig Gdns	40 A3
Earl Haig Homes	42 B6
Earlston Pl	45 F1
East Adam St	37 E3
East Broughton Pl 1	40 C6
East Castle Rd	43 H5
East Claremont St	40 C6
East Ct 2	42 D1
East Cromwell St	41 E2
East Crosscauseway	37 E4
Easter Belmont Rd	42 C3
Easter Dalry Dr	43 G4
Easter Dalry Pl 1	43 G3
Easter Dalry Rigg 3	43 G4
Easter Dalry Rd	43 G3
Easter Dalry Wynd	43 G3
Easter Drylaw Av	38 D5
Easter Drylaw Bk	38 D4
Easter Drylaw Dr	38 D5
Easter Drylaw Gdns	38 D5
Easter Drylaw Gro	38 D5
Easter Drylaw Ln	38 D5
Easter Drylaw Pl	38 D5
Easter Drylaw Vw	38 D4
Easter Drylaw Way	38 D5
Easter Hermitage	41 G5
Easter Rd	41 F5
Easter Warriston	40 B4
East Fettes Av	39 G5
East Fountainbridge	36 B3
East Hermitage Pl	41 F4
East Lillyput	40 A3
East London St	40 C6
East Mkt St	37 D2
East Mayfield	45 E6
East Montgomery Pl	41 E6
East Newington Pl	44 D5
East Norton Pl	37 F1
East Parkside	37 F4
East Pilton Fm Av	39 F3
East Pilton Fm Cres	39 G3
East Pilton Fm Rigg	39 F3
East Pilton Fm Wynd	39 G3
East Preston St	44 D5
East Preston St La 3	44 D5
East Restalrig Ter	41 G4
East Sciennes St	44 D5
East Scotland St La	40 C6
East Silvermills La	40 A6
East Trinity Rd	40 A3
East Werberside	39 F4
East Werberside Pl	39 F4
Edina Pl	41 E6
Edina St	41 E6
Edinburgh Dock	41 G2
Edmonstones Cl 5	37 D3
Eglinton Cres	43 G3
Eglinton St 3	43 F3
Eildon St	40 B5
Eildon Ter	40 A5
Elbe St	41 F3
Elder St	37 D1
Elder St E 5	37 D1
Elgin Pl	43 G3
Elgin St	41 E6
Elgin St N	41 E6
Elgin Ter	41 E6
Elizafield	40 D4
Ellersly Rd	42 C3
Elliot St	41 E6
Elm Pl 2	41 G4
Elm Row	40 D6
Elmwood Ter	41 G4
Eltringham Gdns	42 D6
Eltringham Gro	42 D6
Eltringham Ter	42 D6
Esdaile Bk	44 C6
Esdaile Gdns	44 C6
Esdaile Pk 1	44 C6
Esplanade	36 C3
Eton Ter	36 A1
Ettrickdale Pl	40 A5
Ettrick Gro	43 H5
Ettrick Ln	43 G6
Ettrick Rd	43 G6
Eyre Cres	40 B6
Eyre Pl	40 B6
Eyre Pl La	40 B6
Eyre Ter	40 B6

F

Name	Ref
Falcon Gdns	44 A6
Ferryfield	39 G4
Ferry Gait Cres	38 B4
Ferry Gait Dr	38 B4
Ferry Gait Gdns	38 B4
Ferry Gait Pl	38 B4
Ferry Gait Wk	38 B4
Ferrylee	40 D2
Ferry Rd	40 C3
Ferry Rd Av	39 E4
Ferry Rd Dr	39 E3
Ferry Rd Gdns	38 D4
Ferry Rd Gro	38 D4
Ferry Rd Pl	38 D4
Festival Sq 1	36 B3
Fettes Av	39 G6
Fettes Ri	39 G4
Fettes Row	40 B6
Fidra Ct	38 B3
Findhorn Pl	44 D5
Findlay Av	41 H5
Findlay Cotts	41 H5
Findlay Gdns	41 H5
Findlay Gro	41 H5
Findlay Medway	41 H5
Fingal Pl	44 C5
Fingzies Pl 3	41 G4
Fishmarket Sq 2	39 E1
Fleshmarket Cl 13	37 D2
Forbes Rd	44 A6
Forbes St	37 E4
Ford's Rd	42 C6
Forrest Hill	37 D3
Forrest Rd	37 D3
Forth Ind Est	39 F1
Fort Ho	40 D2
Forth St	37 D1
Forthview Rd	38 D6
Forthview Ter	38 C6
Fountainbridge	36 B4
Fowler Ter	43 G4
Fox St	41 G3
Fraser Av	39 H3
Fraser Cres	39 H3
Fraser Gdns	39 H3
Fraser Gro	39 H3
Frederick St	36 C1

G

Name	Ref
Gabriel's Rd 6	37 D1
Gabriel's Rd (Stockbridge) 6	40 A6
Gardiner Gro	38 C6
Gardiner Rd	38 C6
Gardiner Ter	42 C1
Gardner's Cres	36 A3
Garscube Ter	43 E2
Gayfield Cl	40 D6
Gayfield Pl	40 D6
Gayfield Pl La	40 D6
Gayfield Sq	40 D6
Gayfield St	40 C6
Gayfield St La	40 C6
Gentle's Entry 8	37 F2
George IV Br	37 D2
George Sq	37 D4
George Sq La	37 D4
George St	36 B2

Gibbs Entry	37 E3	Grays Ct **6**	37 E3	Hawthorn Ter **5**	36 A2	Howe St	36 C1	Kimmerghame Vw	39 F5

Gibbs Entry 37 E3
Gibson St 40 D4
Gibson Ter 36 A4
Gifford Pk 37 E3
Giles St 41 E3
Gillespie Cres 36 B4
Gillespie Pl 36 B4
Gillespie St 36 B4
Gillsland Pk 43 G6
Gillsland Rd 43 G6
Gilmore Pk 36 A4
Gilmore Pl 43 H5
Gilmour's Entry **7** 37 E3
Gilmour St 37 E3
Gladstone Pl 41 G4
Gladstone Ter 44 D5
Glanville Pl **5** 40 A6
Glenarm Pl 40 C1
Glencairn Cres 43 G3
Glendevon Av 42 C4
Glendevon Gdns 42 C4
Glendevon Gro 42 C5
Glendevon Pk 42 C5
Glendevon Pl 42 C4
Glendevon Rd 42 C5
Glendevon Ter 42 C4
Glenfinlas St 36 B2
Glengyle Ter 36 B4
Glenlea Cotts 42 D6
Glenlee Av 45 H2
Glenlee Gdns 45 H2
Glenogle Ct 40 A5
Glenogle Pl **7** 40 A6
Glenogle Rd 40 A6
Glenogle Ter 40 A5
Glenorchy Pl **4** 37 E1
Glenorchy Ter 45 E6
Glen St 36 C3
Gloucester La 36 B1
Gloucester Pl 36 B1
Gloucester Sq 36 B1
Gloucester St 36 B1
Goldenacre Ter 40 A4
Gordon St 41 F4
Gorgie Cotts 42 D6
Gorgie Pk Cl 43 E6
Gorgie Pk Rd 43 E5
Gorgie Rd 43 E5
Gosford Pl 40 C3
Graham St 40 D3
Grandfield 40 B3
Grandville 40 B2
Grange Ct 44 D5
Grange Cres 44 C6
Grange Ln 44 B6
Grange Ln Gdns 44 C6
Grange Rd 44 C5
Granton Cres 39 G2
Granton Gdns 39 G2
Granton Gro 39 G2
Granton Mains Av 38 D2
Granton Mains Bk **1** 38 D2
Granton Mains Brae 38 D2
Granton Mains Ct 39 E2
Granton Mains E 39 E2
Granton Mains Gait 38 D2
Granton Mains Vale 38 D2
Granton Mains Wynd 38 D2
Granton Medway 39 F2
Granton Mill Cres 38 D2
Granton Mill Dr 38 D2
Granton Mill March 38 C3
Granton Mill Pk 38 C2
Granton Mill Pl 38 C2
Granton Mill Rd 38 C2
Granton Mill W **1** 38 C3
Granton Pk Av 39 F1
Granton Pier 39 G1
Granton Pl 39 G2
Granton Rd 39 G2
Granton Sq 39 G1
Granton Ter 39 G2
Granton Vw 39 G1
Grantully Pl 45 E6
Granville Ter 43 H5
Grassmarket 36 C3

Grays Ct **6** 37 E3
Gray's Ln 43 F6
Great Junct St 41 E3
Great King St 36 C1
Great Michael Cl **4** 40 C1
Great Michael Ri 40 C2
Great Michael Sq **1** 40 C1
Great Stuart St 36 A2
Green, The 38 A4
Greendale Pk 38 B4
Greenhill Ct 44 A5
Greenhill Gdns 44 A5
Greenhill Pk 44 A6
Greenhill Pl 44 A6
Greenhill Ter 44 A5
Greenside End **6** 37 E1
Greenside La 37 E1
Greenside Pl **5** 37 E1
Greenside Row 37 E1
Green St 40 C6
Greyfriars Pl 37 D3
Grierson Av 39 H2
Grierson Cres 39 H2
Grierson Gdns 39 H2
Grierson Rd 39 G2
Grierson Sq 39 H2
Grierson Vil 39 H2
Grigor Av 39 E5
Grigor Dr 39 E5
Grigor Gdns 39 E5
Grigor Ter 39 E5
Grindlay St 36 B3
Grindlay St Ct 36 B3
Groathill Av 38 D6
Groathill Gdns E 38 D6
Groathill Gdns W 38 D6
Groathill Ln 38 D5
Groathill Rd N 38 D5
Groathill Rd S 38 D6
Grosvenor Cres 43 G3
Grosvenor Gdns 43 G3
Grosvenor St 36 A3
Grove St 36 A3
Grove Ter **4** 36 A3
Guardianswood 42 D3
Gullan's Cl 37 E2
Gunnet Ct 38 B3
Guthrie St 37 D3

H
Haddington Pl 40 D6
Haddon's Ct 37 E3
Hailes St 36 B4
Halmyre St 41 E5
Hamburgh Pl **1** 40 D2
Hamilton Pl 40 A6
Hamilton's Folly Ms **5** 37 E4
Hamilton Wynd 40 D2
Hammermen's Entry 37 E2
Hampton Pl **4** 43 F3
Hampton Ter 43 F3
Hanover St 36 C1
Harden Pl 43 G5
Hardwell Cl 37 E4
Harrismith Pl 41 F6
Harrison Gdns 43 G5
Harrison La 43 G5
Harrison Pl 43 F6
Harrison Rd 43 F5
Hartington Gdns 43 H5
Hartington Pl 43 H5
Hart St 40 C6
Hart St La 40 C6
Hatton Pl 44 C5
Haugh St 40 A6
Hawkhill 41 G5
Hawkhill Av 41 F5
Hawkhill Cl 41 F5
Hawkhill Ct 41 G5
Hawthornbank La 36 A2
Hawthornbank Pl 40 C2
Hawthornbank Ter **2** 40 D2
Hawthorn Bldgs **2** 43 G2
Hawthornden Pl 40 D5

Hawthorn Ter **5** 36 A2
Hawthornvale 40 C2
Haymarket 36 A3
Haymarket Ter 43 G3
Haymarket Yards 43 G3
Hazelbank Ter 43 F6
Henderland Rd 43 E3
Henderson Gdns **4** 41 E3
Henderson Pl 40 B6
Henderson Pl La 40 A6
Henderson Row 40 A6
Henderson St 41 E3
Henderson Ter 43 G5
Heriot Br 36 C3
Heriot Cross **1** 36 C3
Heriot Hill Ter 40 B5
Heriot Pl 36 C3
Heriot Row 36 B1
Hermand Cres 43 F6
Hermand St 43 E6
Hermand Ter 43 E6
Hermitage Pk 41 G5
Hermitage Pk Gro 41 G5
Hermitage Pk Lea 41 G5
Hermitage Pk S 41 G5
Hermitage Pl 41 F4
Hermits Cft 37 F4
Heron Pl 39 G1
Hesperus Crossway 39 G1
High Riggs 36 C3
High Sch Yards 37 E3
High St 37 D2
Hillend Pl **10** 41 H1
Hillhouse Rd 38 A5
Hillpark Av 38 A5
Hillpark Brae 42 A1
Hillpark Ct 38 A5
Hillpark Cres 38 A6
Hillpark Dr 38 A5
Hillpark Gdns 38 A6
Hillpark Grn 38 A6
Hillpark Gro 38 A6
Hillpark Ln 38 B6
Hillpark Ri 38 A6
Hillpark Rd 38 A6
Hillpark Ter 38 A6
Hillpark Way 38 B6
Hillpark Wd 38 B6
Hill Pl 37 E3
Hillside Cres 40 D6
Hillside St 41 E6
Hill Sq 37 E3
Hill St 36 B1
Hill St La N 36 B1
Hill St La S 36 C2
Hillview 38 C6
Hollybank Ter 43 F6
Holyrood Ct 37 F2
Holyrood Pk 45 F2
Holyrood Pk Rd 45 E5
Holyrood Rd 37 E2
Home St 36 B4
Hopefield Ter 40 D2
Hope Pk Cres 37 E4
Hope Pk Sq **1** 37 E4
Hope Pk Ter 37 E4
Hope St 36 B2
Hope St La 36 B2
Hope Ter 44 B6
Hopetoun Cres 40 D6
Hopetoun St 40 D6
Horne Ter 36 A4
Horse Wynd 37 F2
House o'Hill Av 38 B5
House o'Hill Brae 38 B5
House o'Hill Cres 38 B5
House o'Hill Gdns 38 C5
House o'Hill Grn 38 B5
House o'Hill Gro 38 B5
House o'Hill Pl 38 B5
House o'Hill Rd 38 B5
House o'Hill Row 38 B5
House o'Hill Ter 38 C6
Howard Pl 40 B5
Howard St 40 B5
Howden St 37 E3

Howe St 36 C1
Hugh Miller Pl 40 A6
Hunter's Cl **13** 36 C3
Hunter Sq 37 D2
Huntingdon Pl 40 D6
Hutchison Ho 40 B5
Hutchison Crossway 42 D6
Hutchison Medway 43 E6
Hutchison Pk 42 D6
Hutchison Rd 42 D6
Hutchison Vw 42 D6
Hutton Cl 37 F2
Hutton Rd 37 F2

I
Imperial Dock 41 F1
Inchcolm Ct 38 D3
Inchgarvie Ct 38 D4
Inchkeith Ct 40 D5
Inchmickery Ct 38 B3
India Bldgs **3** 37 D3
India Pl 36 B1
India St 36 B1
Industrial Rd 41 F4
Industry Home **1** 40 D3
Industry La 40 D3
Infirmary St 37 E3
Inglis Ct **2** 36 C3
Inverleith Av 40 A4
Inverleith Av S 40 A4
Inverleith Gdns 39 H4
Inverleith Gro 39 G5
Inverleith Pl 39 H4
Inverleith Pl La 40 A4
Inverleith Row 40 A4
Inverleith Ter 40 A5
Inverleith Ter La 40 A5
Iona St 41 E5
Iona St La 41 E5
Ivy Ter 43 F5

J
Jackson's Entry **7** 37 F2
Jamaica Ms 36 B1
Jamaica St 36 B1
Jamaica St N La 36 B1
Jamaica St S La 36 B1
Jamaica St W **2** 36 B1
James' Ct **4** 37 D2
James Craig Wk 37 D1
Jameson Pl 41 E5
Jane St 41 E4
Jane Ter **2** 45 F1
Jawbone Wk 37 D4
Jeffrey Av 42 C1
Jeffrey St 37 D2
Jessfield Ter 40 C2
John Cotton Business Cen 41 F6
John's La 41 F3
John's Pl 41 F4
Johnston Ter 36 C3
Junction Pl 41 E4

K
Kaimes Ct 42 A4
Keir St 36 C3
Keith Cres 42 C1
Keith Row 42 D1
Keith Ter 42 C1
Kemp Pl 40 A6
Kenmure Av 45 H2
Kerr St 40 A6
Kew Ter 43 F3
Kilgraston Ct 44 B6
Kilgraston Rd 44 C6
Kilmaurs Rd 45 F6
Kilmaurs Ter 45 F6
Kimmerghame Dr 39 F4
Kimmerghame Ln 39 F4
Kimmerghame Path 39 F4
Kimmerghame Pl 39 F5
Kimmerghame Row 39 F4
Kimmerghame Ter 39 F4

Kimmerghame Vw 39 F5
Kincaid's Ct 37 D3
Kinellan Gdns 42 D3
Kinellan Rd 42 D2
Kinghorn Pl 40 C3
King's Br 36 C3
Kingsburgh Cres 39 F1
Kingsburgh Rd 42 D3
Kings Haugh 45 H6
King's Meadow 45 G6
King's Stables La 36 C3
King's Stables Rd 36 C3
King St 41 E3
Kinnear Ri 39 G4
Kinnear Rd 39 G4
Kirkgate 41 F3
Kirkhill Dr 45 F6
Kirkhill Gdns 45 F5
Kirkhill Rd 45 F5
Kirkhill Ter 45 F5
Kirk St 41 E4
Kirkwood Pl **3** 45 F1
Kittle Yards 44 D5
Kyle Pl 37 F1

L
Ladehead 40 C4
Lady Lawson St 36 C3
Lady Menzies Pl 45 F1
Lady Stair's Cl **6** 37 D2
Lady Wynd 36 C3
Lamb's Cl **2** 37 E4
Lamb's Ct **1** 40 B1
Lansdowne Cres 43 G3
Lapicide Pl 40 D3
Largo Pl 40 D3
Lauderdale St 44 B5
Lauder Ln 44 D6
Lauder Rd 44 C5
Laurel Ter **1** 43 F5
Laurie St 41 F4
Lauriston Gdns 36 C3
Lauriston Pk 36 C4
Lauriston Pl 36 B4
Lauriston St 36 C3
Lauriston Ter 36 C3
Laverockbank Av 40 B2
Laverockbank Cres 40 B2
Laverockbank Gdns 40 B2
Laverockbank Gro 40 B2
Laverockbank Rd 40 B2
Laverockbank Ter 40 B2
Lawnmarket 37 D2
Leamington La 36 B4
Leamington Pl 36 B4
Leamington Rd 36 A4
Leamington Ter 36 B4
Learmonth Av 39 G6
Learmonth Ct 43 G1
Learmonth Cres 43 G1
Learmonth Gdns 43 G1
Learmonth Gdns La 43 G1
Learmonth Gdns Ms 36 A1
Learmonth Gro 39 G6
Learmonth Pk 39 G6
Learmonth Pl 39 G6
Learmonth Ter 43 G1
Learmonth Ter La 43 G1
Learmonth Vw **1** 36 A1
Leith Docks 41 F4
Leith Links 41 F4
Leith St 37 D1
Leith Wk 40 D6
Lennel Av 40 A2
Lennox Row 40 A2
Lennox St 36 A1
Lennox St La 36 A1
Leopold Pl 40 D6
Leslie Pl 39 H6
Leven Cl **1** 36 B4
Leven St 36 B4
Leven Ter 36 C4
Lewis Ter **12** 36 A3
Liddesdale Pl 40 A5
Lilyhill Ter 45 H1

Street	Page	Grid
Lily Ter 1	43	F6
Limes, The	43	H6
Lindean Pl	41	G4
Lindsay Pl	40	D2
Lindsay Rd	40	C1
Lindsay St	40	D2
Links Gdns	41	G3
Links Gdns La	41	G3
Links La 3	41	F3
Links Pl	41	F3
Linksview Ho	41	E3
Lismore Av	45	H1
Lismore Cres	45	H1
Little King St	37	D1
Livingstone Pl	44	C5
Lixmount Av	40	B2
Lixmount Gdns	40	B2
Loaning Mills	41	H6
Loaning Rd	41	H6
Lochend Av	41	G6
Lochend Castle Barns	41	G6
Lochend Cl	37	F2
Lochend Cres	41	H6
Lochend Dr	41	G6
Lochend Gdns	41	G6
Lochend Gro	41	H6
Lochend Ho	41	H6
Lochend Pk	41	G6
Lochend Quad	41	H6
Lochend Rd	41	G5
Lochend Rd S	41	G6
Lochend Sq	41	G6
Lochinvar Pl	39	G1
Lochrin Bldgs	36	B4
Lochrin Pl	36	B4
Lochrin Ter 3	36	B4
Loch Rd	38	B6
Lochview Ct	37	F2
Loganlea Dr	45	H1
Loganlea Gdns	41	H6
Logan St	40	B6
Logie Grn Gdns	40	B5
Logie Grn La	40	B5
Logie Grn Rd	40	B5
Logie Mill	40	B5
Lomond Rd	40	A2
London Rd	37	E1
London St	40	C6
Long Craig Rigg	38	D1
Long Craig Rd	38	D1
Lonsdale Ter	36	C4
Lord Russell Pl 1	44	D5
Lorne Pl	41	E5
Lorne Sq	41	E5
Lorne St	41	E5
Lothian Rd	36	B2
Lothian St	37	D3
Lovers' Ln		
Lower Gilmore Pl	36	A4
Lower Granton Rd	39	
Lower London Rd	45	F1
Lufra Bk	39	H2
Lutton Pl	37	E4
Lynedoch Pl	36	A2
Lynedoch Pl La	36	A2
Lyne St	41	F1
M		
McDonald Pl	40	C5
McDonald Rd	40	C5
McDonald St	40	D5
McKelvie Par	40	A1
Mackenzie Pl	36	B1
McLaren Rd	45	F6
McLaren Ter 11	36	A3
McLeod St	43	F4
McNeill St	36	A4
Madeira Pl	40	D3
Madeira St	40	D2
Magdala Cres	43	G3
Magdala Ms	43	G3
Maidencraig Ct	38	D6
Maidencraig Cres	38	D6
Maidencraig Gro	38	D6
Main Pt	36	C3
Main St	38	A5
Malta Grn 2	40	A6
Malta Ter	40	A6
Manderston St	41	E4
Manor Pl	36	A2
Mansfield Pl	40	C6
Mansionhouse Rd	44	C5
Marchfield Gro	38	B5
Marchfield Pk	38	A5
Marchfield Pk La	38	A5
Marchfield Ter	38	B6
March Gait	38	A6
March Gro	38	A6
Marchhall Cres	45	F5
Marchhall Pl	45	F5
Marchhall Rd	45	F5
Marchmont Cres	44	B5
Marchmont Rd	44	B5
Marchmont St	44	B5
March Pines	38	A6
March Rd	38	A6
Mardale Cres	43	H6
Marine Dr	38	B2
Marine Esplanade	41	H3
Marionville Av	41	G6
Marionville Cres	41	H6
Marionville Dr	41	H6
Marionville Gro	41	H6
Marionville Medway 1	41	H6
Marionville Pk	41	G6
Marionville Rd	41	F6
Marischal Pl 1	42	D1
Maritime La	41	F3
Maritime St	41	F3
Market St	37	D2
Marshall's Ct 3	37	E1
Marshall St 2	37	E3
Martello Ct	38	B3
Maryfield	37	F1
Maryfield Pl	45	F1
Mary's Pl 1	39	H6
May Ct	38	B3
Mayfield Gdns	45	E6
Mayfield Gdns La	45	E6
Mayfield Rd	45	E6
Mayfield Ter	45	E6
Mayville Gdns	40	B2
Mayville Gdns E	40	B2
Meadowbank	45	G1
Meadowbank Av	45	G1
Meadowbank Cres	45	G1
Meadowbank Pl 7	45	H1
Meadowbank Ter	45	G1
Meadow La	37	D4
Meadow Pl	36	C4
Meadow Pl La	44	C5
Melbourne Pl 7	37	D2
Melgund Ter	40	C6
Melville Cres	36	A2
Melville Dr	36	C4
Melville Pl 6	36	A2
Melville St	36	A2
Melville St La	36	A2
Melville Ter	44	C5
Mentone Gdns	45	E6
Merchant St	37	D3
Merchiston Av	43	H5
Merchiston Bk Av	43	H6
Merchiston Bk Gdns	43	H6
Merchiston Cres	43	H6
Merchiston Gro	43	F5
Merchiston Ms	43	H5
Merchiston Pk	43	H5
Merchiston Pl	43	H6
Mertoun Pl	43	G5
Meuse La	37	D2
Middleby St	45	E6
Middlefield	40	D5
Middle Meadow Wk	37	D4
Middle Pier	39	G1
Mid Gillsland Rd	43	G6
Millerfield Pl	44	C5
Miller Row	36	A2
Mill La	41	E3
Milnacre	40	C4
Milton St	45	F1
Minto St	45	E5
Mitchell St	41	F3
Moat Dr	43	E6
Moat Ho	43	E6
Moat Pl	43	E6
Moat St	43	E6
Moat Ter	43	E6
Moncrieff Ter	44	D5
Monkwood Ct	44	C6
Monmouth Ter	40	A3
Montague St	37	E4
Montagu Ter	40	A4
Montgomery St	40	D6
Montgomery St La	40	D6
Montpelier	43	H5
Montpelier Pk	43	H5
Montpelier Ter	43	H5
Montrose Ter	37	F1
Moray Pk	45	F1
Moray Pk Ter	45	F1
Moray Pl	36	B1
Morningside Rd	43	H6
Morrison Circ	36	A3
Morrison Cres	36	A3
Morrison Link	36	A3
Morrison St	36	A3
Moston Ter	45	E6
Mound, The	36	C2
Mound Pl	36	C2
Mount Gra	44	B6
Muirdale Ter 1	38	C6
Muirhouse Av	38	C4
Muirhouse Av N	38	C3
Muirhouse Bk	38	C4
Muirhouse Cl	38	B3
Muirhouse Ct	38	B3
Muirhouse Cres	38	B3
Muirhouse Dr	38	B3
Muirhouse Gdns	38	B3
Muirhouse Grn	38	C4
Muirhouse Gro	38	B3
Muirhouse Ln	38	C3
Muirhouse Medway	38	B3
Muirhouse Pk	38	B4
Muirhouse Parkway	38	C3
Muirhouse Pl E	38	C4
Muirhouse Pl W	38	C4
Muirhouse Ter	38	B4
Muirhouse Vw	38	B3
Muirhouse Way	38	C4
Mulberry Pl 1	40	C3
Multrees Wk	37	D1
Munro Pl 1	40	B5
Murano Pl	41	E6
Murdoch Ter	36	A4
Murieston Cres	43	G4
Murieston Cres La 2	43	G4
Murieston La	43	G4
Murieston Pl	43	G4
Murieston Rd	43	G4
Murieston Ter	43	F4
Murrayfield Av	43	E3
Murrayfield Dr	42	D3
Murrayfield Gdns	42	E2
Murrayfield Pl 1	43	E3
Murrayfield Rd	42	D2
Myrtle Ter	43	F5
N		
Napier Ln	43	G6
Napier Rd	43	G6
Nelson Pl 1	36	C1
Nelson St	36	C1
Nether Bakehouse 9	37	F2
Netherby Rd	39	H3
Nether Craigwell	37	F1
New Arthur Pl	37	E3
New Arthur St 5	37	E3
Newbattle Ter	44	A6
New Bells Ct 4	41	F3
New Broompark	39	F1
New Broughton	40	C6
New Cut Rigg	40	C3
Newhaven Main St	40	B1
Newhaven Pl	40	C1
Newhaven Rd	40	D4
Newington Rd	44	D5
New John's Pl	37	E4
Newkirkgate 2	41	E4
Newlands Pk	45	E6
New La	40	C2
New Orchardfield	41	E4
New Skinner's Cl	37	E2
News Steps	37	D2
New St	37	E2
Newton St	43	F5
Nichollfield	40	C2
Nicolson Sq	37	D3
Nicolson St	37	E3
Niddry St	37	D2
Niddry St S 3	37	E3
Nightingale Way	36	C4
Nisbet Ct	41	G5
Noble Pl	41	G4
North Bk St	37	D2
North Br	37	D2
North Br Arc 10	37	D2
North Castle St	36	B1
North Charlotte St	36	B1
North Clyde St La 1	37	D1
Northcote St	43	G4
North E Circ Pl	36	B1
North Fort St	40	D2
North Junct St	40	D2
North Leith Mill 4	40	D2
North Leith Sands	40	D2
North Meadow Wk	36	C4
North Pk Ter	39	H6
North Richmond St 1	37	E3
North St. Andrew La	37	D1
North St. Andrew St	37	D1
North St. David St	37	D1
Northumberland Pl 2	36	C1
Northumberland Pl La	36	C1
Northumberland St	36	C1
Northumberland St N E La	36	C1
Northumberland St S E La	36	C1
Northumberland St S W La	36	C1
Northview Ct	38	C3
North Werber Pk	39	F5
North Werber Pl	39	F4
North Werber Rd	39	F5
North W Circ Pl	36	B1
Norton Pk	41	F6
O		
Oakfield Pl	37	E3
Oakville Ter	41	G4
Ocean Dr	40	D2
Ocean Way	41	F2
Ogilvie Ter	43	F6
Old Assembly Cl 9	37	D2
Old Broughton 2	40	C6
Old Ch La	45	H4
Old Fishmarket Cl	37	D2
Old Tolbooth Wynd	37	E2
Orchard Bk	43	F1
Orchard Brae	39	G6
Orchard Brae Av	43	F1
Orchard Brae Gdns	43	F1
Orchard Brae Gdns W	43	F1
Orchard Brae W	39	G6
Orchard Cres	43	E1
Orchard Dr	43	E1
Orchardfield La	41	E5
Orchard Gro	39	G6
Orchard Pl	39	F6
Orchard Rd	43	F1
Orchard Rd S	43	E1
Orchard Ter	43	F1
Orchard Toll	43	F1
Ormidale Ter	42	D3
Orwell Pl	43	G4
Orwell Ter	43	G4
Osborne Ter	43	F3
Oxcars Ct	38	B3
Oxcraig St	39	G1
Oxford St	37	F4
Oxford Ter	36	A1
P		
Paisley Cres	45	H2
Paisley Gdns	45	H2
Paisley Ter	45	H2
Palmerston Pl	36	A2
Palmerston Pl La	36	A3
Palmerston Rd	44	C5
Panmure Pl	36	C4
Papermill Wynd	40	D5
Pape's Cotts	43	E3
Park Pl	40	B2
Park Rd	40	B2
Parkside St	37	F4
Parkside Ter	37	F4
Parkvale Pl	41	G4
Parliament Sq	37	D2
Parliament St	41	E3
Parsons Grn Ter 2	45	H1
Patrick Geddes Steps 14	36	C3
Patriothall 3	40	A6
Pattison St	41	F3
Peacock Ct	40	C1
Peel Ter	45	E6
Peffermill Ind Est	45	H6
Pembroke Pl	43	F3
Pennywell Cotts	38	C2
Pennywell Ct	38	C3
Pennywell Gdns	38	B3
Pennywell Gro	38	C3
Pennywell Medway	38	B3
Pennywell Pl	38	C3
Pennywell Rd	38	C3
Pennywell Vil	38	D2
Persevere Ct	41	E2
Perth St	40	A6
Picardy Pl	37	F1
Pier Pl	40	B1
Piershill La 3	45	H1
Piershill Pl 4	45	H1
Piershill Sq W	45	H1
Pilrig Cotts	41	E5
Pilrig Gdns	40	D4
Pilrig Glebe	41	E5
Pilrig Hts	40	C4
Pilrig Ho Cl	40	D4
Pilrig Ind Est	40	D4
Pilrig Pl	41	E5
Pilrig St	40	D4
Pilton Av	39	E3
Pilton Cres	39	G3
Pilton Dr	39	F3
Pilton Dr N	39	F2
Pilton Gdns	39	F3
Pilton Ln	39	F3
Pilton Pk	39	F3
Pilton Pl	39	F3
Pinkhill	42	A4
Pinkhill Pk	42	A4
Pirniefield Bk	41	H4
Pirniefield Gdns	41	H4
Pirniefield Gro	41	H4
Pirniefield Pl	41	H4
Pirniefield Ter	41	H4
Pirrie St	41	E4
Pitlochry Pl	41	F6
Pitsligo Rd	44	A6
Pitt St	40	C3
Playfair Steps 1	36	C2
Pleasance	37	E3
Pollard Glebe	42	B6
Polwarth Cres	43	H5
Polwarth Gdns	43	G5

Polwarth Gro 43 G6
Polwarth Pk 43 G5
Polwarth Pl 43 G5
Polwarth Ter 43 G6
Ponton St 36 B4
Poplar La 41 F3
Porterfield Rd 39 F5
Portgower Pl 39 H6
Port Hamilton 36 B3
Portland Gdns 40 D2
Portland Row 40 D2
Portland St 40 D2
Portland Ter 3 40 D2
Portsburgh Sq 5 36 C3
Potterrow 37 D3
Powderhall Brae 40 C4
Powderhall Rigg 40 C4
Powderhall Rd 40 C4
Prestonfield Av 45 F6
Prestonfield Bk 45 F6
Prestonfield Cres 45 F6
Prestonfield Gdns 45 F6
Prestonfield Rd 45 F6
Prestonfield Ter 45 F6
Priestfield Av 45 G6
Priestfield Cres 45 G6
Priestfield Gdns 45 G6
Priestfield Gro 45 G6
Priestfield Rd 45 F6
Priestfield Rd N 45 F5
Primrose Bk Rd 40 A2
Primrose St 41 F4
Primrose Ter 43 F5
Prince of Wales
  Dock 41 E1
Prince Regent St 40 D2
Princes St 36 C2
Prospect Bk Cres 41 G4
Prospect Bk Gdns 41 G5
Prospect Bk Gro 41 H4
Prospect Bk Pl 41 G4
Prospect Bk Rd 41 G4
Prospect Bk Ter 41 H4

Q
Quality St 38 A5
Quality St La 38 A5
Quarry Cl 37 E4
Quayside Mills 3 41 E3
Quayside St 41 E3
Queen Charlotte La 41 F3
Queen Charlotte St 41 F3
Queen's Av 38 C6
Queen's Av S 38 D6
Queen's Cres 45 E6
Queen's Dr 37 F2
Queensferry Rd 43 G1
Queensferry St 36 A2
Queensferry St La 36 A2
Queensferry Ter 43 F1
Queen's Gdns 38 D6
Queen's Pk Av 45 G1
Queen's Pk Ct 45 H2
Queen's Rd 38 D6
Queen St 36 B1
Queen St Gdns E 36 C1
Queen St Gdns W 36 C1
Quilts, The 40 D3
Quilts Wynd 40 D3

R
Raeburn Ms 39 H6
Raeburn Pl 39 H6
Raeburn St 39 H6
Ramsay Gdn 36 C2
Ramsay La 36 C2
Randolph Cliff 36 A2
Randolph Cres 36 A2
Randolph La 36 B2
Randolph Pl 36 B2
Rankeillor St 37 E4
Ratcliffe Ter 44 D5
Ravelston Ct 43 E2
Ravelston Dykes 43 E2
Ravelston Dykes La 42 B2

Ravelston Dykes Rd 42 C1
Ravelston Gdn 42 D2
Ravelston Hts 42 C1
Ravelston Ho Gro 42 C1
Ravelston Ho Ln 42 D1
Ravelston Ho Pk 42 D1
Ravelston Ho Rd 42 D1
Ravelston Pk 43 F2
Ravelston Pl 4 43 G2
Ravelston Ri 42 D2
Ravelston Ter 43 G1
Redbraes Gro 40 C4
Redbraes Pl 40 C4
Reekie's Ct 37 E3
Regent Br 2 37 D1
Regent Pl 45 F1
Regent Rd 37 E2
Regent's Ct 1 37 F1
Regent Ter 37 F1
Regent Ter Ms 37 F1
Register Pl 37 D1
Reid's Cl 37 F2
Reid's Ct 1 37 F2
Reid Ter 39 H6
Rennie's Isle 41 E2
Restalrig Av 45 H1
Restalrig Circ 41 H5
Restalrig Cres 41 H5
Restalrig Dr 41 H6
Restalrig Gdns 41 H6
Restalrig Ho 41 H6
Restalrig Pk 41 G5
Restalrig Rd 41 G4
Restalrig Rd S 45 H1
Restalrig Sq 41 H5
Restalrig Ter 41 F4
Richmond La 37 E3
Richmond Pl 37 E3
Richmond Ter 36 A3
Riego St 36 B3
Rillbank Cres 44 C5
Rillbank Ter 44 C5
Rintoul Pl 40 A6
Ritchie Pl 43 G5
Riversdale Cres 42 D4
Riversdale Gro 42 D3
Riversdale Rd 42 C3
Robb's Ln 42 D6
Robb's Ln Gro 42 D6
Robertson Av 43 E5
Robertson Gait 43 E6
Robertson's Cl 37 E3
Robertson's Ct 2 37 F2
Rocheid Pk 39 G4
Rocheid Path 40 A5
Rochester Ter 43 H6
Rodney Pl 40 B6
Rodney St 40 B5
Romero Pl 45 E5
Ronaldson's Wf 41 E3
Rope Wk 36 A4
Rosebank Cotts 36 A3
Rosebank Gdns 39 H3
Rosebank Gro 39 H3
Rosebank Rd 39 H3
Rosebery Cres 43 G3
Rosebery Cres La 43 G3
Roseburn Av 43 E3
Roseburn Cliff 43 E3
Roseburn Cres 43 E4
Roseburn Dr 43 E3
Roseburn Gdns 2 43 E3
Roseburn Maltings 43 F3
Roseburn Pl 43 E3
Roseburn St 43 E4
Roseburn Ter 43 F3
Rosemount Bldgs 36 A3
Roseneath Pl 44 B5
Roseneath St 44 C5
Roseneath Ter 44 C5
Rose Pk 40 A3
Rose St 36 B2
Rose St N La 36 B2
Rose St S La 36 B2
Rosevale Pl 1 41 G4
Rosevale Ter 41 F4

Roseville Gdns 40 B2
Rossie Pl 41 E6
Rosslyn Cres 40 D5
Rosslyn Ter 40 D5
Rothesay Ms 43 G2
Rothesay Pl 43 G2
Rothesay Ter 43 G2
Roxburgh Pl 37 E3
Roxburgh St 37 E3
Royal Circ 36 B1
Royal Cres 40 B6
Royal Pk Pl 45 G1
Royal Pk Ter 45 G1
Royal Ter 37 E1
Royal Ter Ms 37 F1
Royston Mains Av 39 F2
Royston Mains Cl 39 F2
Royston Mains Cres 39 F2
Royston Mains Gdns 39 F2
Royston Mains Grn 39 F2
Royston Mains Pl 39 E2
Royston Mains Rd 39 F2
Royston Mains St 39 E2
Royston Ter 40 A4
Russell Gdns 43 F3
Russell Pl 40 A2
Russell Rd 43 F3
Rutland Ct 2 36 B3
Rutland Ct La 36 B3
Rutland Pl 1 36 B2
Rutland Sq 36 B2
Rutland St 36 B2
Ryehill Av 41 G4
Ryehill Gdns 41 G4
Ryehill Gro 41 G4
Ryehill Pl 41 G4
Ryehill Ter 41 G4

S
St. Andrew Pl 41 F4
St. Andrew Sq 37 D1
St. Anthony La 41 E3
St. Anthony Pl 5 41 E3
St. Anthony St 6 41 E3
St. Bernard's Cres 36 A1
St. Bernard's Row 40 A6
St. Catherine's Gdns 42 B4
St. Catherine's Pl 44 D5
St. Clair Av 41 F5
St. Clair Pl 41 F5
St. Clair Rd 41 F5
St. Clair St 41 F5
St. Colme St 36 B2
St. David's Pl 9 36 A3
St. David's Ter 10 36 A3
St. Giles' St 37 D2
St. James' Pl 37 D1
St. James Sq 37 D1
St. John's Cres 42 A4
St. John's Hill 9 37 E3
St. John St 37 E2
St. Leonard's Bk 37 F4
St. Leonard's Crag 1 37 F4
St. Leonard's Hill 37 E4
St. Leonard's La 37 E4
St. Leonard's St 37 E4
St. Margaret's Pl 44 B6
St. Margaret's Rd 44 A6
St. Mary's St 37 E2
St. Ninian's Row 3 37 D1
St. Patrick Sq 37 E4
St. Patrick St 3 37 E4
St. Peter's Bldgs 36 A4
St. Peter's Pl 36 A4
St. Stephen Pl 40 A6
St. Stephen St 40 A6
St. Teresa Pl 43 G6
St. Thomas Rd 44 C6
St. Triduana's Rest 41 H6
St. Vincent Pl 40 A6
St. Vincent St 40 B6
Salamander Ct 41 G3
Salamander Pl 41 G3
Salamander St 41 F3
Salamander Yards 41 H3

Salisbury Ms 45 E5
Salisbury Pl 44 D5
Salisbury Rd 45 E5
Salmond Pl 45 F1
Saltire Sq 39 E1
Saltire St 39 E1
Salvesen Cres 38 B2
Salvesen Gdns 38 C2
Salvesen Gro 38 C2
Salvesen Ter 38 C2
Sandpiper Rd 40 C1
Sand Port 41 F2
Sandport Pl 41 E2
Sandport St 41 E2
Sandport Way 41 E3
Sauchiebank 43 F4
Saughton Av 42 D5
Saughton Cres 42 C4
Saughton Gdns 42 C4
Saughton Gro 42 C4
Saughtonhall Av 42 C4
Saughtonhall Av W 42 C4
Saughtonhall Circ 42 C4
Saughtonhall Cres 42 C4
Saughtonhall Dr 42 C3
Saughtonhall Gdns 42 D4
Saughtonhall Gro 42 D4
Saughtonhall Pl 42 C4
Saughtonhall Ter 42 C4
Saughton Ln 42 C4
Saughton Mains Av 42 A6
Saughton Mains Bk 42 A6
Saughton Mains
  Ind Est 42 A6
Saughton Mains Pk 42 A6
Saughton Mains St 42 A6
Saughton Mains Ter 42 A6
Saughton Pk 42 C4
Saughton Rd 42 A6
Saunders St 36 B1
Saxe-Coburg Pl 40 A6
Saxe-Coburg St 40 A6
Saxe-Coburg Ter 4 40 A6
Sciennes 44 D5
Sciennes Gdns 44 D5
Sciennes Hill Pl 44 D5
Sciennes Pl 2 44 D5
Sciennes Ho Pl 44 D5
Sciennes Rd 44 C5
Scone Gdns 45 H1
Scotland St 40 B6
Seacot 1 41 H4
Seafield Av 41 H4
Seafield Pl 41 H4
Seafield Rd 41 H4
Seaforth Dr 38 D6
Seaforth Ter 38 D6
Sealcarr St 39 F1
Seaport St 5 41 F3
Semple St 36 B3
Seton Pl 44 D5
Shaftesbury Pk 43 F6
Shandon Cres 43 F6
Shandon Pl 43 F6
Shandon Rd 43 F6
Shandon St 43 F6
Shandon Ter 43 F6
Shandwick Pl 36 A3
Shaw's Pl 40 D5
Shaw's Sq 2 40 D6
Shaw's St 40 D5
Shaw's Ter 40 D5
Sheriff Bk 41 E3
Sheriff Brae 41 E3
Sheriff Pk 41 E3
Shore 41 F3
Shore Pl 41 F3
Shrub Pl 40 D5
Shrub Pl La 40 D5
Sienna Gdns 44 D5
Silverknowes Bk 38 A4
Silverknowes Brae 38 A4
Silverknowes Ct 38 A4
Silverknowes Cres 38 A3
Silverknowes Dell 38 B4
Silverknowes Dr 38 A4

Silverknowes
  Eastway 38 A4
Silverknowes Gdns 38 A3
Silverknowes Grn 38 B4
Silverknowes Gro 38 A3
Silverknowes Hill 38 A4
Silverknowes
  Midway 38 B4
Silverknowes Neuk 38 B5
Silverknowes
  Parkway 38 A3
Silverknowes Pl 38 A3
Silverknowes Rd 38 A4
Silverknowes Rd E 38 A4
Silverknowes Rd S 38 A5
Silverknowes
  Southway 38 B4
Silverknowes Vw 38 B4
Silvermills 40 A6
Simon Sq 4 37 E3
Simpson Ln 36 C4
Sinclair Cl 2 43 F6
Sinclair Gdns 43 F5
Sinclair Pl 43 E5
Slateford Gait 43 E6
Slateford Grn 43 E6
Slateford Rd 43 E6
Slateford Rd Br 43 G5
Slater's Steps 6 37 F2
Sleigh Dr 41 G6
Sleigh Gdns 41 H6
Sloan St 41 E5
Smithfield St 43 E5
Smith's Pl 41 E4
Solicitor's Bldgs 4 37 D3
Somerset Pl 41 F4
South Beechwood 42 B4
South Br 37 D2
South Charlotte St 36 B2
South Clerk St 37 E4
South Coll St 37 D3
South E Circ Pl 1 36 B1
South Ettrick Rd 43 F5
South Fort St 40 D3
South Gayfield La 40 D6
South Gillsland Rd 43 G6
South Gray's Cl 37 E2
South Gray St 45 E6
South Groathill Av 38 D6
South Lauder Rd 44 D6
South Laverockbank
  Av 40 B2
South Learmonth Av 43 G1
South Learmonth
  Gdns 43 G1
South Lorne Pl 41 E5
South Meadow Wk 36 C4
South Oxford St 45 E5
South Pk 40 B2
South St. Andrew St 37 D1
South St. David St 37 D1
South Sloan St 41 E5
South Trinity Rd 40 A3
Spencer Pl 40 A2
Spence St 45 E5
Spey St 40 D5
Spey St La 40 D5
Spey Ter 40 D5
Spier's Pl 7 41 E3
Spittalfield Cres 37 E4
Spittal St 36 B3
Spittal St La 3 36 C3
Spottiswoode Rd 43 H6
Spottiswoode St 44 B5
Springfield 40 D4
Springfield Bldgs 3 41 E4
Springfield La 41 E4
Springfield St 41 E4
Spring Gdns 45 F1
Springwell Pl 43 G4
Spylaw Rd 43 G6
Stafford St 36 A2
Stair Pk 42 D3
Stanhope Pl 43 F3
Stanhope St 43 F3
Stanley Pl 45 F1

Stanley Rd 40 B2
Stanwell St 40 D4
Starbank Rd 40 B2
Stead's Pl 41 E4
Stenhouse Av 42 B5
Stenhouse Av W 42 B6
Stenhouse Cotts 42 B6
Stenhouse Cres 42 B6
Stenhouse Cross 42 B6
Stenhouse Dr 42 B6
Stenhouse Gdns 42 B6
Stenhouse Gdns N 42 B6
Stenhouse Gro 42 B6
Stenhouse Pl E 42 B6
Stenhouse Pl W 42 B6
Stenhouse St E 42 B6
Stenhouse St W 42 A6
Stenhouse Ter 42 C6
Stevenlaw's Cl 37 D2
Stevenson Av 42 D5
Stevenson Dr 42 B6
Stevenson Gro 42 D5
Stevenson Rd 42 D5
Stevenson Ter 42 D5
Stewartfield 40 C4
Stewart Ter 43 E5
Stirling Rd 40 A2
Strachan Gdns 38 B6
Strachan Rd 42 C1
Strathearn Pl 44 A6
Strathearn Rd 44 B6
Succoth Av 43 E2
Succoth Ct 43 E2
Succoth Gdns 43 E2
Succoth Pk 42 D2
Succoth Pl 43 E2
Summerbank 40 B6
Summerfield Gdns 41 G4
Summerfield Pl 41 G4
Summerhall 4 44 D5
Summerhall Cres 4 37 E4
Summerhall Pl 5 44 D5
Summerhall Sq 44 D5
Summer Pl 40 B5
Summerside Pl 40 C3
Summerside St 40 C3
Sunbury Ms 43 G2
Sunbury Pl 43 G2
Sunbury St 43 G2
Sunnybank Pl 45 G1
Sunnybank Ter 4 45 F1
Sunnyside 41 F6
Surrey Pl 2 43 F3
Sutherland St 43 F3
Swanfield 41 E3
Sylvan Pl 44 C5

T
Tanfield 40 B5
Tantallon Pl 44 D5
Tarvit St 36 B4
Taylor Gdns 41 E3
Taylor Pl 45 F1
Tay St 43 G5
Telfer Sub 43 G4
Telford Dr 39 E5
Telford Gdns 39 E5
Telford Gro 39 E4
Telford March 39 E5
Telford Pl 39 E5
Telford Rd 39 E6
Temple Pk Cres 43 G5
Tennant St 41 E4
Terrars Cft 37 F4
Teviotdale Pl 40 A6
Teviot Pl 37 D3
Thirlestane La 44 B6
Thirlestane Rd 44 B5
Thistle Ct 3 36 C1
Thistle Pl 36 A4
Thistle St 36 C1
Thistle St N E La 36 C1
Thistle St N W La 36 C1
Thistle St S E La 36 C1

Thistle St S W La 36 C1
Thomson's Ct 8 36 C3
Thorntreeside 41 F4
Thorntreeside
  Ind Est 41 F5
Thorntree St 41 E4
Thornville Ter 41 F5
Thornybauk 36 B3
Timber Bush 41 F2
Tinto Pl 40 D4
Tipperlinn Rd 43 H6
Tolbooth Wynd 41 E3
Torphichen Pl 36 A3
Torphichen St 36 A3
Tower Pl 41 F2
Tower St 41 F2
Tower St La 41 F2
Tower Wynd 41 F2
Townswomen's
  Guild Wk 37 D4
Trafalgar La 40 C3
Trafalgar St 40 D3
Traquair Pk E 42 A4
Trinity Ct 39 H3
Trinity Cres 40 A1
Trinity Gro 40 A2
Trinity Mains 40 A3
Trinity Rd 40 A2
Trinity Way 40 A3
Tron Sq 12 37 D2
Tynecastle La 43 F5
Tynecastle Ter 43 F5
Tytler Ct 45 F1
Tytler Gdns 37 F1

U
Ulster Cres 45 H2
Ulster Dr 45 H2
Union Pl 2 37 E1
Union St 40 C6
Upper Bow 8 37 D2
Upper Coltbridge
  Ter 43 E2
Upper Damside 43 G2
Upper Dean Ter 36 A1
Upper Gilmore Pl 36 B4
Upper Gilmore Ter 36 B4
Upper Gray St 44 D5
Upper Greenside
  La 37 E1
Upper Gro Pl 36 A4
Upper Hermitage 41 F4

V
Valleyfield St 36 B4
Vanburgh Pl 41 F4
Veitch's Sq 40 A6
Vennel 36 C3
Ventnor Pl 45 F6
Ventnor Ter 45 E6
Victoria Dock 41 F2
Victoria Pk Neuk 40 C3
Victoria Quay 41 E2
Victoria St 37 D3
Victoria Ter 9 36 C3
Viewcraig Gdns 37 E3
Viewcraig St 37 E2
Viewforth 36 A4
Viewforth Gdns 44 A5
Viewforth Sq 43 H5
Viewforth Ter 43 H5
Violet Ter 43 F5
Vivian Ter 38 A5

W
Walker St 36 A2
Walker Ter 6 36 A3
Warden's Cl 37 D3
Wardie Av 39 H3
Wardieburn Dr 39 G2
Wardieburn Pl E 39 G2
Wardieburn Pl N 39 G2
Wardieburn Pl S 39 G2
Wardieburn Pl W 39 F2
Wardieburn Rd 39 F2

Wardieburn St E 39 G2
Wardieburn St W 39 F2
Wardieburn Ter 39 F2
Wardie Cres 39 G2
Wardie Dell 39 H2
Wardiefield 39 G2
Wardie Gro 39 G2
Wardie Ho La 39 H1
Wardie Pk 39 H3
Wardie Rd 39 H3
Wardie Sq 39 H2
Wardie Steps 39 H2
Wardlaw Pl 43 F5
Wardlaw St 43 F5
Wardlaw Ter 43 F5
Warrender Pk Cres 44 A5
Warrender Pk Rd 44 B5
Warrender Pk Ter 44 B5
Warriston Av 40 B4
Warriston Cres 40 B5
Warriston Dr 40 A4
Warriston Gdns 40 A4
Warriston Gro 40 A4
Warriston Pl 40 B5
Warriston Rd 40 B3
Warriston's Cl 15 37 D2
Warriston Ter 40 A4
Washington La 43 G4
Washington St 43 G4
Waterfront Av 39 E1
Waterfront Bdy 39 E2
Waterfront Gait 38 C2
Waterfront Pk 38 D2
Waterloo Pl 37 D1
Water's Cl 6 41 F3
Water St 41 F3
Watson Cres 43 G5
Waverley Bri 37 D2
Waverley Pk 45 F1
Waverley Pk Ter 45 F1
Waverley Pl 45 F1
Waverley St 37 D2
Websters Land 10 36 C3
Well Ct 4 36 A2
Wellington Pl 41 F3
Wellington St 41 E6
Wemyss Pl 36 B1
Wemyss Pl Ms 36 B1
Werberside Ms 39 F4
West Adam St 37 E3
West Annandale St 40 C5
West App Rd 36 B3
West Bow 37 D3
West Bowl Grn St 40 D3
West Bryson Rd 43 G5
West Castle Rd 43 H5
West Catherine Pl 43 F3
West Cherrybank 40 B2
West Coates 43 F3
West Coll St 37 D3
West Ct 42 D1
West Cromwell St 1 41 E2
West Crosscauseway 37 E4
West End 36 B2
West End Pl 43 G4
Wester Cl 3 40 C1
Wester Coates Av 43 F3
Wester Coates Gdns 43 F3
Wester Coates Pl 43 F2
Wester Coates Rd 43 F3
Wester Coates Ter 43 F3
Wester Drylaw Av 38 C5
Wester Drylaw Dr 38 B5
Wester Drylaw Pk 38 D5
Wester Drylaw Pl 38 C5
Wester Drylaw Row 38 D6
Western Cor 42 C3
Western Gdns 42 D3
Western Harbour 40 D1
Western Harbour Dr 40 C1
Western Pl 42 D3
Western Ter 42 D3
West Ferryfield 39 G3
Westfield Av 42 D5
Westfield Ct 42 D5

Westfield Rd 43 E5
Westfield St 43 E5
West Fountain Pl 43 G4
West Gorgie Pk 42 D6
West Gra Gdns 44 C6
West Granton
  Access 39 G2
West Granton Rd 39 F2
Westhall Gdns 44 A5
West Harbour Rd 39 F1
West Maitland St 36 A3
West Mayfield 45 E6
West Mill La 36 A2
West Montgomery
  Pl 40 D6
West Newington Pl 44 D5
West Nicolson St 37 E3
West Norton Pl 37 F1
West Pk Pl 43 G3
West Pier 39 F1
West Pilton Av 38 D4
West Pilton Bk 38 C3
West Pilton Brae 39 E3
West Pilton Cres 38 C3
West Pilton
  Crossway 38 D3
West Pilton Dr 38 D3
West Pilton Gdns 38 D3
West Pilton Grn 38 D3
West Pilton Gro 38 D3
West Pilton Lea 38 D3
West Pilton Ln 38 D3
West Pilton March 39 E2
West Pilton Pk 38 D3
West Pilton Pl 39 E3
West Pilton Ri 38 D3
West Pilton Rd 39 E3
West Pilton St 38 D3
West Pilton Ter 38 D3
West Pilton Vw 38 D4
West Pilton Way 39 E3
West Port 36 C3
West Preston St 44 D5
West Register St 37 D1
West Register St
  La 4 37 D1
West Richmond St 37 E3
West Scotland St La 40 B6
West Shore Business
  Cen 38 D1
West Shore Rd 38 C2
West Shore Rd
  Trd Est 38 D1
West Silvermills La 40 A6
West Stanhope Pl 1 43 F3
West Tollcross 36 B4
West Werberside 39 F4
West Winnelstrae 39 G4
West Wds 39 F5
Wheatfield Pl 43 E5
Wheatfield Rd 43 E5
Wheatfield St 43 F5
Wheatfield Ter 1 43 E5
Whitehall Ct 38 C6
White Horse Cl 37 F2
Whitehouse Ln 44 A5
Whitehouse Ter 44 B6
White Pk 43 F5
Whitingford 40 C3
Whitson Cres 42 C5
Whitson Gro 42 C5
Whitson Pl E 42 C5
Whitson Pl W 42 C5
Whitson Rd 42 C5
Whitson Ter 42 C5
Whitson Wk 42 B5
Whitson Way 42 C5
Whyte Pl 45 F1
Wilfrid Ter 5 45 H1
William St 36 A2
William St La N E 36 A2
William St La N W 36 A2
William St La S E 36 A2
William St La S W 36 A3
Willowbank Row 40 C2

Willowbrae Av 45 H2
Willowbrae Rd 45 H2
Wilson's Ct 3 37 E2
Windmill Cl 37 E4
Windmill La 37 D4
Windmill Pl 6 37 E4
Windmill St 37 D4
Windrush Dr 40 C1
Windsor St 40 D6
Windsor St La 40 D6
Wishaw Ter 45 G1
Wolseley Cres 45 H1
Wolseley Gdns 8 45 H1
Wolseley Pl 9 45 H1
Wolseley Ter 6 45 H1
Woodbine Ter 41 F5
Woodville Ter 41 F5
Wright's Hos 44 A5
Wyvern Pk 44 C6

Y
Yardheads 41 E3
Yeaman La 43 G4
Yeaman Pl 43 G4
York Bldgs 7 37 D1
York La 37 D1
York Pl 37 D1
York Rd 40 A2
Young St 36 B2
Young St La N 36 B2
Young St La S 36 B2

Z
Zetland Pl 40 A2

EDINBURGH

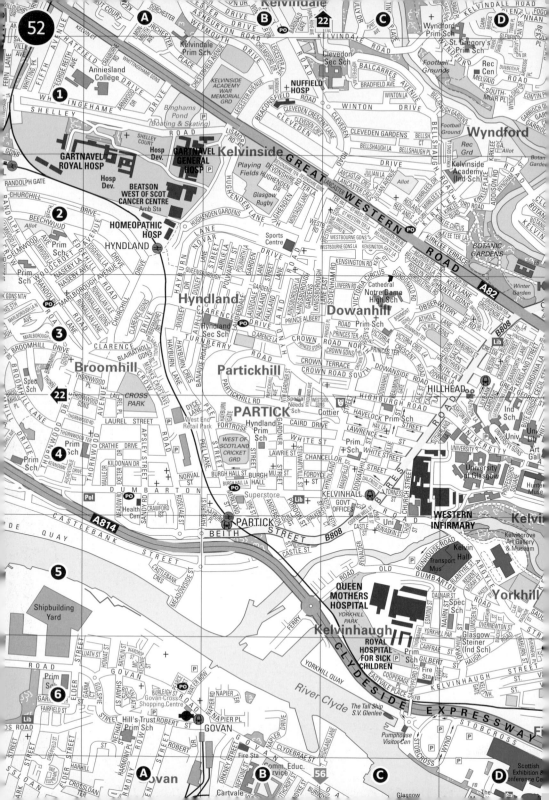

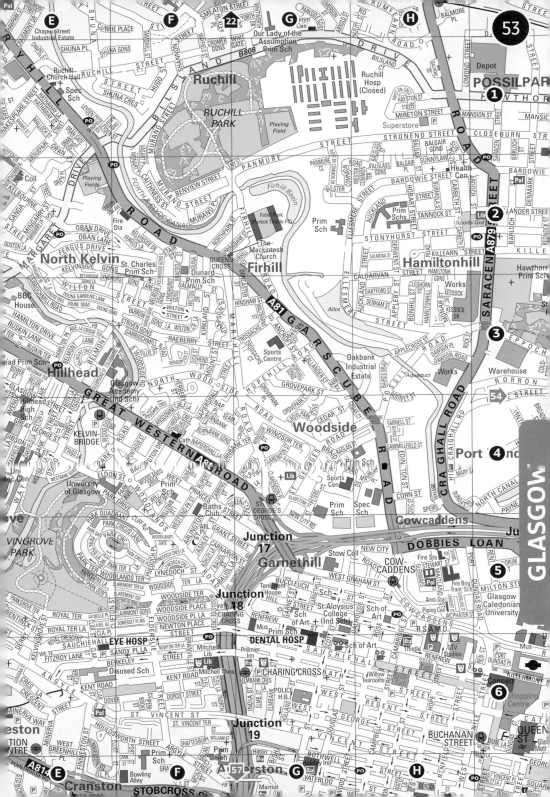

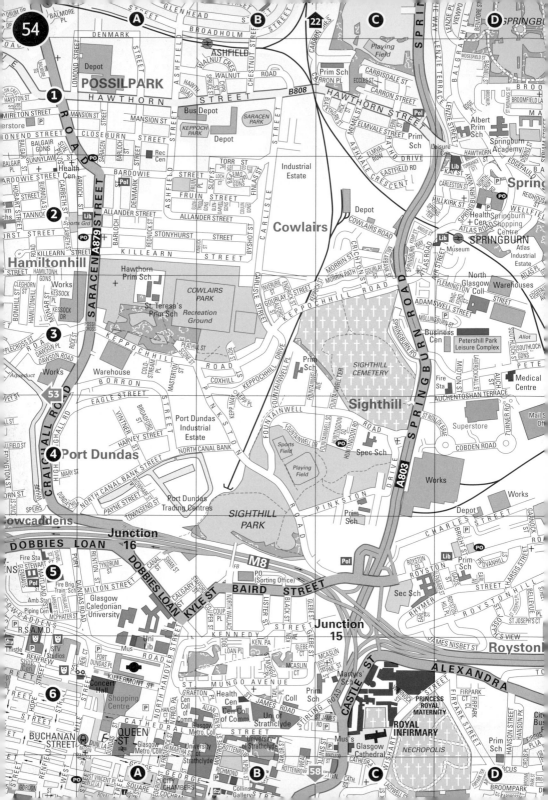

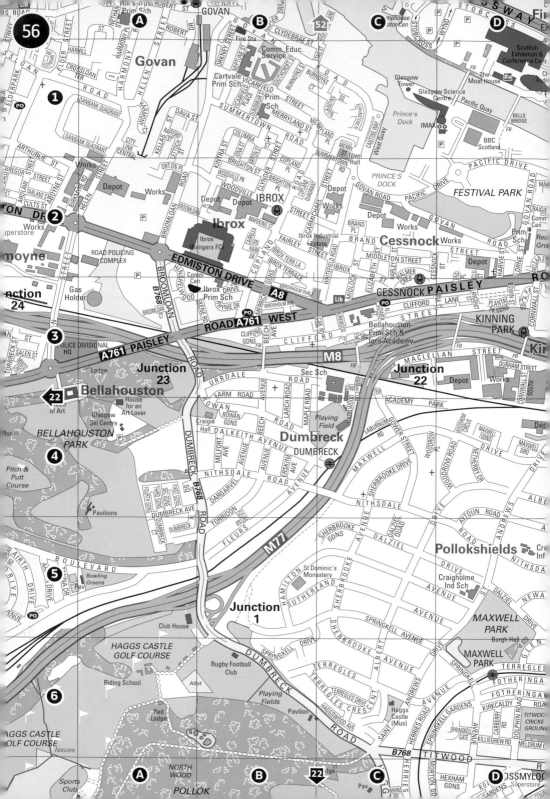

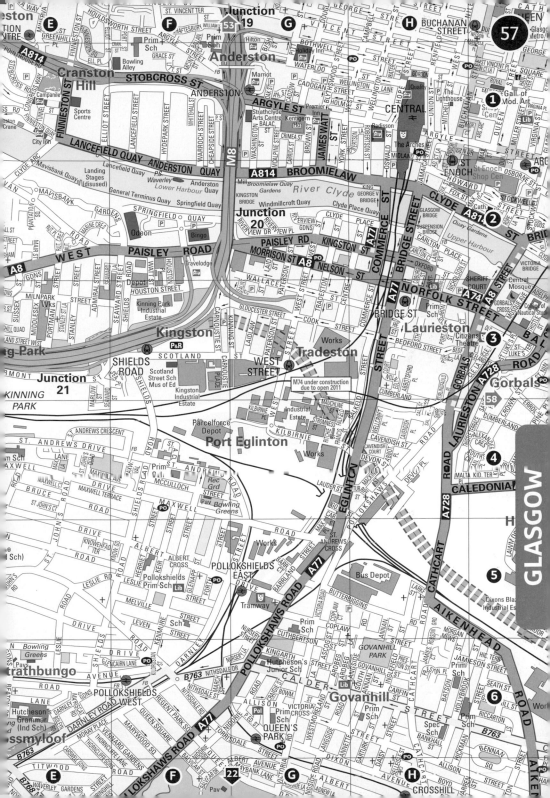

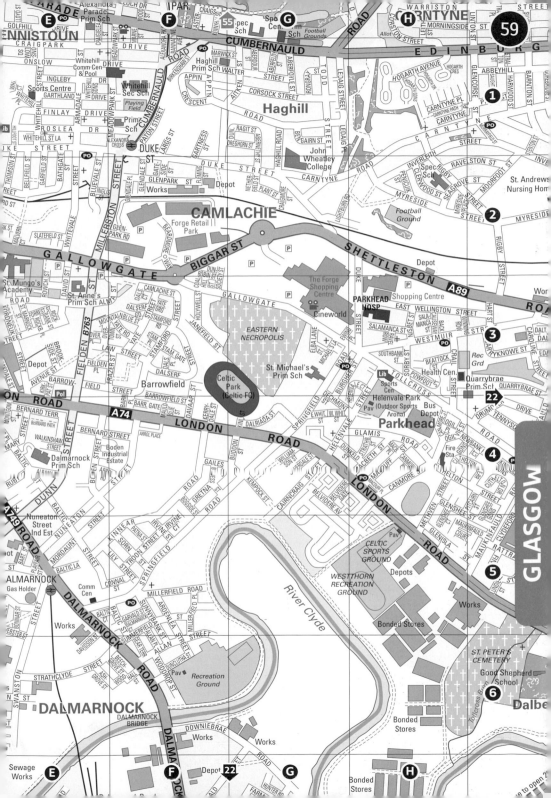

This index contains streets that are not named on the map due to insufficient space. For each of these cases the nearest street that does appear on the map is shown in *italics*.

A

Abbotsford Pl 57 H3
Abercromby Dr 58 D2
Abercromby Sq 58 D2
Abercromby St 58 D3
Aberdour St 59 G1
Aberfeldy St 59 G1
Aberfoyle St 59 G1
Abernethy St 59 G1
Academy Pk 56 C4
Acorn Ct 58 D4
Acorn St 58 D4
Adams Ct La 57 H2
Adamswell St 54 C3
Addison Rd 52 D2
Adelphi St 58 B3
Admiral St 57 E3
Aikenhead Rd 57 H5
Aird's La
 off Bridgegate 58 A2
Airlie La 52 B2
Airlie St 52 A3
Aitken St 59 G1
Albany St 59 E4
Albert Br 58 A3
Albert Cross 57 F5
Albert Dr 56 C6
Albion Gate
 off Albion St 58 B1
Albion St 58 B2
Alexander Cres 58 A4
Alexandra Ct 55 F6
Alexandra Cross 59 F1
Alexandra Par 54 C6
Alexandra Pk St 59 F1
Alford St 54 B3
Alfred La 52 D3
Alfred Ter 53 E3
Allander St 54 A2
Allan Glen Pl 54 B6
Allan Pl 59 F5
Allan St 59 F6
Allison Pl
 *off Prince Edward
 St* 57 G6
Allison St 57 G6
Alma St 59 E3
Almond St 55 H5
Alston La
 *off Claythorn
 St* 58 C2
Amisfield St 53 E1
Anchor La
 *off St. Vincent
 Pl* 58 A1
Ancroft St 53 G3
Anderson St 52 B4
Anderston Cross
 Cen 57 G1
Anderston Quay 57 F2
Angus St 54 C2
Annandale St 57 H5
Annbank Pl 58 D2
Annbank St 58 D2
Annette St 57 G6
Annfield Pl 58 D1
Anson St 58 D4
Anthony St 57 G1
Appin Cres 59 F1
Appin Rd 59 F1
Appleby St 53 H3
Applecross St 53 H3
Apsley La
 off Apsley St 52 A4
Apsley St 52 A4
Arcadia Pl 58 C3
Arcadia St 58 C3
Ardbeg La 57 G6
Ardbeg St 57 G6
Ardenlea St 59 F5

Ardery St
 off Apsley St 52 A4
Ardessie Pl 52 D1
Ardoch St 54 A2
Ardo Gdns
 *off Hinshelwood
 Dr* 56 A3
Argyle St 57 G1
Argyll Arc 58 A1
Ark La 58 D1
Arlington Pl 53 F5
Arlington St 53 F5
Armadale Ct 55 E6
Armadale Path 55 E6
Armadale Pl 55 E6
Armadale St 59 E1
Armour St 58 C2
Arnwood Dr 52 A1
Arrol Pl 59 F4
Arrol Rd 59 E4
Arthur St 52 D5
Ascog St 57 G6
Ashfield St 54 A2
Ashgrove St 59 E6
Ashley La 53 F5
Ashley St 53 F5
Ashton La 52 D4
Ashton La N
 off Ashton La 52 D4
Ashton Rd 52 D4
Ashvale Cres 54 C1
Aspen Dr 55 E3
Athole Gdns 52 C3
Athole La 52 C3
Atlas Ind Est 54 D2
Atlas Pl 54 D3
Atlas Rd 54 C2
Atlas Sq
 off Ayr St 54 D2
Auchentoshan
 Ter 54 D4
Auchinloch St 54 D3
Auckland St 53 H3
Avenuepark St 53 E2
Avenue St 59 E3
Avonspark St 55 E3
Ayr St 54 C3
Aytoun Rd 56 D5

B

Back Causeway 59 H3
Bagnell St 54 D1
Bain Sq
 off Bain St 58 C2
Bain St 58 C2
Bairds Brae 53 H3
Baird St 54 B5
Balaclava St
 off McAlpine St 57 G1
Balcarres Av 52 C1
Balgair Pl 53 H2
Balgair St 53 H1
Balglass Gdns 53 H2
Balglass St 53 H2
Balgraybank St 54 D2
Balgrayhill Rd 54 D1
Baliol La 53 F5
Baliol St 53 F5
Ballantrae Ct 57 F1
Ballater Pl 58 B4
Ballater St 58 A3
Ballindalloch Dr 55 E6
Ballindarroch La
 off Armadale St 55 E6
Balmore Sq 53 H1
Balornock Rd 55 E1
Baltic Ct
 off Baltic St 59 E5
Baltic La 59 E5
Baltic Pl 59 E4

Baltic St 59 E4
Banavie La
 off Banavie Rd 52 B3
Banavie Rd 52 A3
Bankhall St 57 H6
Bank St 53 E4
Bannatyne Av 59 F1
Barbreck Rd
 *off Pollokshaws
 Rd* 57 G6
Barclay St
 off Lenzie St 54 D1
Bardowie St 53 H2
Bargeddie St 55 H4
Barloch St 54 A2
Barmulloch Rd 55 E2
Barnhill Dr
 *off Foresthall
 Dr* 55 E3
Barrack St 58 C2
Barrington Dr 53 F4
Barrland St 57 G5
Barrowfield St 59 E3
Barr St 53 G3
Bartholomew St 59 E5
Bathgate St 59 E2
Bath La
 *off Wellington
 St* 53 G6
Bath La W
 off North St 53 F6
Bath St 53 G6
Batson St 57 H6
Beaconsfield Rd 52 B3
Beardmore Way 59 F2
Beaton Rd 57 E6
Beattock St 59 H3
Beaumont Gate 52 C3
Bedford La 57 H3
Bedford St 57 H3
Beech Av 56 B3
Beechgrove St 59 F6
Beith St 52 B5
Belgrave La 53 E3
Belgrave Ter 53 E3
Belhaven Cres La
 *off Kensington
 Rd* 52 C2
Belhaven Ter 52 C2
Belhaven Ter La 52 C2
Belhaven Ter W 52 C2
Belhaven Ter W
 La 52 C2
Bellevue Pl 54 D5
Bellfield St 59 E2
Bellgrove St 58 D2
Bellshaugh Ct 52 C1
Bellshaugh Gdns 52 C1
Bellshaugh La 52 C1
Bellshaugh Pl 52 C1
Bellshaugh Rd 52 C1
Bell St 58 B2
Belmont Cres 53 E3
Belmont La 53 E3
Belmont St 53 E3
Beltane St
 off Dorset St 53 F6
Benalder St 52 C5
Bengairn St 59 G1
Bennan Sq 58 A6
Benny Lynch Ct 58 A3
Benthall St 58 B4
Bentinck St 53 E5
Benview St 53 F2
Berkeley St 53 E6
Berkeley Ter La
 off Elderslie St 53 F6
Bernard Path 59 E4
Bernard St 59 E4
Bernard Ter 59 E4

Berryburn Rd 55 G2
Biggar St 59 F2
Bilsland Ct 53 H1
Bilsland Dr 53 F1
Binnie Pl 58 C3
Birchend Dr 55 F4
Birchend Pl 55 E4
Birch St
 off Silverfir St 58 B5
Birkenshaw St 59 F1
Birkwood St
 *off Dalmarnock
 Rd* 59 F6
Birnam Rd
 off London Rd 59 H5
Birnie Ct 55 G3
Birnie Rd 55 G2
Bishopmill Pl 55 G2
Bishopmill Rd 55 G1
Bishop St 57 G1
Blackburn St 56 D2
Blackfriars St 58 B1
Blackie St 52 D6
Black St 54 B5
Blackthorn St 54 C1
Blairatholl Av 52 A3
Blairatholl Gdns 52 A3
Blantyre St 52 D5
Blochairn Rd 55 E5
Bluevale St 59 E2
Blythswood Ct
 off Cadogan St 57 G1
Blythswood Sq
 *off Blythswood
 St* 53 G6
Blythswood St 57 G1
Boden Ind Est 59 E4
Boden St 59 E4
Boghead Rd 55 E1
Bogside St 59 F4
Boleyn Rd 57 E6
Bonawe St
 off Kirkland St 53 F2
Boness St 59 F4
Bonhill St 53 H3
Bonnar St 59 E5
Borron St 54 A3
Botanic Cres 52 D2
Botanic Cres La 52 D2
Bothwell La
 *off Blythswood
 St* 57 G1
Bothwell St 53 G6
Boundary Rd
 *off Rutherglen
 Rd* 58 C6
Bower St 53 E3
Bowman St 57 G6
Bowmont Gdns 52 C3
Bowmont Ter 52 C3
Bradfield Av 52 C1
Braehead St 58 B5
Braemore Gdns 54 B2
Braeside St 53 F3
Braid Sq 53 G4
Braid St 53 G4
Brandon St 58 D2
Brand Pl 56 C2
Brand St 56 C2
Breadalbane St
 *off St. Vincent
 St* 53 F6
Brechin St 53 G6
Bridgegate 58 A2
Bridgegate Path
 off Bridgegate 58 A2
Bridge St 57 H2
Bridgeton Business
 Cen 58 D3
Bridgeton Cross 58 D3

Brighton Pl 56 B2
Brighton St 56 B2
Bright St 54 D5
Briton St 56 B2
Broadford St 54 A4
Broad St 58 D3
Brodick St 55 E5
Brookside St 59 E3
Brook St 58 D3
Broomfield La 54 D1
Broomfield Pl 54 D1
Broomfield Rd 54 D1
Broomielaw 57 G2
Broomknowes Rd 55 E2
Broomloan Ct 56 A3
Broomloan Circ 54 D6
Broomloan Rd 56 A2
Broompark Circ 54 D6
Broompark Dr 58 D1
Broompark La 58 D1
Broompark St 58 D1
Brora La
 off Brora St 55 H5
Brora St 55 H5
Brown St 57 G1
Bruce Rd 57 E4
Brunswick St 58 A1
Buccleuch La
 off Rose St 53 G5
Buccleuch St 53 G5
Buchanan St 57 H1
Buchan St
 off Norfolk St 57 H3
Buckingham St 52 D3
Buckingham Ter 52 D3
Bucksburn Rd 55 G2
Buddon St 59 G4
Bunhouse Rd 52 C5
Burgher St 59 G3
Burgh Hall La 52 B4
Burgh Hall St 52 B4
Burgh La 52 D3
Burleigh St 52 A6
Burmola St 53 H2
Burnbank Gdns 53 F4
Burnbank La
 *off Napiershall
 St* 53 F4
Burnbank Pl
 off Drygate 58 C1
Burnbank Pl
 (Woodside)
 *off Burnbank
 Ter* 53 G4
Burnbank Ter 53 F4
Burnbrae St 55 E2
Burndyke Ct 56 B1
Burndyke Sq 56 B1
Burndyke St 56 B1
Burns St 53 H4
Burrells La 58 C1
Bute Gdns 52 D4
Bute La
 *off Great George
 St* 52 D4
Butterbiggins Rd 57 G5
Butterfield Pl
 *off Pollokshaws
 Rd* 57 G5
Byres Rd 52 C4
Byshot St 54 B2

C

Cadogan St 57 G1
Cadzow St 57 G1
Caird Dr 52 B4
Cairncraig St 59 G3
Cairnlea Dr 56 B2
Caithness St 53 F2
Caldarvan St 53 H3

Calder St 57 H6
Caledonia Av 58 A5
Caledonian Cres
off Great Western
Rd 53 E4
Caledonia Rd 57 H4
Caledonia St 58 A5
Caledon La 52 C3
Caledon St 52 C3
Calgary St 54 A5
Callander St 53 G3
Calton Entry
off Gallowgate 58 C2
Cambridge St 53 H6
Camden Ter 58 A4
Camlachie St 59 F3
Camp Rd 58 D6
Campsie St 54 D1
Canal St 54 A5
Candleriggs 58 B2
Canmore Pl 59 H4
Canmore St 59 H4
Canting Way 56 C1
Carberry Rd 56 D6
Carbeth St 53 H2
Carbisdale St 54 C1
Carbrook St 55 E5
Cardarrach St 55 E1
Cardow Rd 55 G2
Cardross Ct 58 D1
Cardross St 58 D1
Cardwell St
off Eglinton St 57 G4
Cardyke St 55 E2
Carfin St 57 H6
Carfrae St 52 C6
Carillon Rd 56 C3
Carleston St 54 D2
Carlisle St 54 B2
Carlton Ct 57 H2
Carlton Pl 57 H2
Carmichael St 56 B2
Carnarvon St 53 F5
Carnoustie Pl 57 F3
Carnoustie St 57 F3
Carntyne Path 59 H1
Carntyne Pl 59 H1
Carntyne Rd 59 G2
Carrick St 57 G2
Carrington St 53 F4
Carron Cres 54 B1
Carron Pl 54 B1
Carron St 54 C1
Carstairs St 59 E6
Castlebank Cres 52 A5
Castle Cres N Ct
off Royal Ex Sq 58 A1
Castle St 54 C6
Castle St (Partick) 52 C5
Cathedral Sq 58 C1
Cathedral St 54 A6
Catherine St
off Hydepark St 57 F1
Cavendish Ct 57 H4
Cavendish Pl 57 H4
Cavendish St 57 H4
Cecil St 52 D3
Cedar Ct 53 G4
Cedar St 53 G4
Central Sta 57 H1
Centre St 57 G3
Cessnock St 56 C2
Chalmers Ct 58 C2
Chalmers Gate
off Claythorn St 58 C2
Chalmers Pl
off Claythorn St 58 C2
Chalmers St 58 C2
Chancellor St 52 B4
Chapel St 53 E1
Chapman St
off Allison St 57 G6
Charing Cross 53 F5

Charing Cross La
off Granville St 53 F6
Charles St 54 C5
Charlotte La
off London Rd 58 B2
Charlotte La S
off Charlotte St 58 B2
Charlotte La W
off London Rd 58 B2
Charlotte St 58 B2
Cheapside St 57 F2
Chelmsford Dr 52 B1
Chesterfield Av 52 A1
Chestnut St 54 B1
Chisholm St 58 B2
Christopher St 55 E4
Church St 52 C4
Circus Dr 58 D1
Circus Pl 58 D1
Circus Pl La 54 D6
City Link Cen 56 A1
Civic St 53 H4
Clairmont Gdns 53 F5
Claremont Pas
off Claremont
Ter 53 F5
Claremont Pl
off Claremont
Ter 53 F5
Claremont St 53 E6
Claremont Ter 53 F5
Claremont Ter La 53 E5
Clarence Dr 52 A3
Clarence Gdns 52 A3
Clarence La 52 B3
Clarendon La
off Clarendon
St 53 G4
Clarendon Pl 53 G4
Clarendon St 53 G4
Clare St 55 E4
Clayslaps Rd 52 D5
Claythorn Av 58 C3
Claythorn Circ
off Claythorn
Av 58 C2
Claythorn Ct
off Claythorn
Pk 58 C2
Claythorn Pk 58 C3
Claythorn St 58 C2
Claythorn Ter
off Claythorn
Pk 58 C2
Clayton Ter 58 D1
Cleghorn St 53 H3
Cleland La 58 A3
Cleland St 58 A3
Clerwood St 59 H2
Cleveden Cres 52 B1
Cleveden Cres La 52 B1
Cleveden Dr 52 B1
Cleveden Dr La
off Mirrlees Dr 52 C2
Cleveden Gdns 52 C1
Cleveland La
off Kent Rd 53 F6
Cleveland St 53 F6
Clifford Gdns 56 B3
Clifford La 56 C3
Clifford Pl
off Clifford St 56 D2
Clifford St 56 B3
Cliff Rd 53 F5
Clifton Pl
off Clifton St 53 E5
Clifton St 53 E5
Closeburn St 54 A1
Clouston Ct
off Fergus Dr 53 E2
Clouston La 53 E2
Clouston St 52 D2

Cloverbank Gdns 55 E5
Cloverbank St 55 E5
Clutha St
off Paisley Rd
W 56 D2
Clydebrae St 52 B6
Clyde Ind Cen 53 E6
Clyde Pl 57 G2
Clydeside
Expressway 52 C6
Clydeside Rd 58 D6
Clyde St 57 H2
Clynder St 56 B2
Coalhill St 59 F3
Cobden Rd 54 D4
Coburg St 57 H3
Cochrane St 58 A1
Cockmuir St 55 E2
Colbert St 58 D5
Coldstream Pl 54 A3
Colebrooke La
off Colebrooke
St 53 E3
Colebrooke Pl 53 E3
Colebrooke St 53 E3
Colebrooke Ter 53 E3
College St 58 B1
Collins St 58 C1
Coll Pl 55 F4
Coll St 55 E4
Columba St 56 B1
Colvend La 58 D5
Colvend St 58 D5
Comelypark Pl
off Comelypark
St 59 E2
Comelypark St 58 D2
Commerce St 57 H3
Commercial Ct 58 B3
Commercial Rd 58 A4
Congress Rd 56 D1
Congress Way 57 E1
Conival St 59 F5
Contin Pl 52 D1
Cook St 57 G3
Cooperage Pl 52 C6
Coopers Well La
off Dumbarton
Rd 52 C5
Coopers Well St 52 C5
Copland Pl 56 B1
Copland Quad 56 B2
Copland Rd 56 B2
Coplaw Ct 57 G5
Coplaw St 57 G5
Cornhill St 55 E1
Corn St 53 H4
Cornwall St 56 D3
Cornwall St S 56 D4
Corsock St 59 G1
Corston St 55 H6
Corunna St 53 E6
Cotton St 58 D6
Coulin Gdns 54 B2
Couper Pl 54 B5
Couper St 54 B5
Coventry Dr 55 F6
Cowan La 53 E4
Cowan St 53 E4
Cowcaddens Rd 53 H5
Cowcaddens St
off Renfield St 53 H5
Cowlairs Rd 54 C2
Coxhill St 54 B3
Craigenbay St 55 F2
Craigendmuir St 55 H4
Craighall Rd 53 H4
Craighead Av 55 H3
Craighall Pl 56 D2
Craighall St
off Craighall
Pl 56 D2
Craigielea St 55 E6

Craigie St 57 G6
Craigmaddie Ter La
off Derby St 53 E5
Craigmont Dr 53 E1
Craigmore St 59 G2
Craignethan Gdns
off Lawrie St 52 B4
Craigpark 59 E1
Craigpark Dr 59 E1
Craigpark Ter
off Craigpark 59 E1
Crail St 59 H3
Cramond St 58 B6
Cranborne Rd 52 A1
Cranston St 53 F6
Cranworth La 52 D3
Cranworth St 52 D3
Crathie Dr 52 A4
Crathie La
off Exeter Dr 52 A4
Crawford La
off Crawford St 52 A4
Crawford Path
off Crawford St 52 A4
Crawford St 52 A4
Cresswell La 52 D3
Cresswell St 52 D3
Crichton Pl
off Crichton St 54 C2
Crichton St 54 C2
Crieff Ct
off North St 53 F6
Crimea St 57 G1
Crinan St 55 F6
Croftbank St 54 D2
Cromer Gdns 53 F1
Cromwell La 53 G4
Cromwell St 53 G4
Crown Circ 52 C3
Crown Ct
off Virginia St 58 A1
Crown Gdns 52 C3
Crown Mans
off North Gardner
St 52 B3
Crownpoint Rd 58 D3
Crown Rd N 52 B3
Crown Rd S 52 B3
Crown St 58 D3
Crown Ter 52 B3
Crow Rd 52 A3
Croy Pl 55 G1
Croy Rd 55 G1
Cubie St 58 D3
Culloden St 55 F6
Cumberland Pl 58 A4
Cumberland St 57 H3
Cumbernauld Rd 59 F1
Custom Ho Quay
off Clyde St 58 A2
Cuthbertson St 57 G6
Cuthelton St 59 H4
Cuthelton Ter 59 H4
Cypress St 54 B1

D

Dalcross La
off Byres Rd 52 C4
Dalcross Pas
off Dalcross St 52 C4
Dalcross St 52 C4
Dale Path 58 D4
Dale St 58 D4
Dalhousie La
off Dalhousie St 53 G5
Dalhousie St 53 G5
Dalintober St 57 G3
Dalkeith Av 56 B4
Dalmally St 53 F3
Dalmarnock Br 59 F6
Dalmarnock Ct 59 F5
Dalmarnock Dr 58 D4
Dalmarnock Rd 58 D4

Dalmeny St 58 C6
Dalnair St 52 C5
Dalnaida St 59 G4
Dalserf Ct 59 F3
Dalserf Gdns 59 F3
Dalserf St 59 F3
Dalziel Dr 56 C5
Dalziel Quad 56 C5
Dargarvel Av 56 B4
Dargarvel Path
off Dumbreck
Av 56 A5
Darnick St 55 F3
Darnley Gdns 57 E6
Darnley Pl
off Darnley Rd 57 E6
Darnley Rd 57 E6
Darnley St 57 F6
Dartford St 53 H3
Davaar St 59 F4
Dava St 56 A1
Davidson St 59 E6
David St 59 E3
Dawson Pl 53 H3
Dawson Rd 53 H3
Deanside La
off Rottenrow 58 B1
Dechmont St 59 G3
Dee St 55 H5
Denham St 53 H3
Denmark St 54 A2
Derby St 53 E6
Derby Ter La 53 E5
Derwent St 53 H2
Deveron St 55 H5
Devon Pl 57 H4
Devonshire Gdns 52 B2
Devonshire Gdns La
off Hyndland
Rd 52 B2
Devonshire Ter 52 B2
Devonshire Ter La 52 B2
Devon St 57 H4
Dick St 53 F3
Dinart St 55 H5
Dinwiddie St 55 G4
Dixons Blazes
Ind Est 58 A5
Dobbies Ln 53 H5
Dobbies Ln Pl 54 B6
Dolphin Rd 56 D6
Doncaster St 53 G2
Don St 55 H6
Dora St 58 D5
Dornoch St 58 D3
Dorset Sq
off Dorset St 53 F6
Dorset St 53 F6
Douglas La
off West Regent
St 53 G6
Douglas St 53 G6
Douglas Ter
off Glencairn Dr 57 F5
Doune Gdns 53 E3
Doune Gdns La 53 E3
Doune Quad 53 E3
Dover St 53 E6
Dowanhill St 52 C3
Dowanside La
off Byres Rd 52 D3
Dowanside Rd 52 C3
Downiebrae Rd 59 F6
Downs St 54 D2
Drake St 58 C3
Dreghorn St 59 G1
Drem Pl
off Merkland St 52 B4
Drumbottie Rd 55 E1
Drumpellier St 55 H4
Drury St
off Renfield St 57 H1

Dryburgh Gdns		Edington St	53 H4	Firpark St	54 D6	Garvald Ct		Granton St	58 C6
off Wilton St	53 F3	Edwin St	56 D3	Firpark Ter	58 D1	*off Baltic St*	59 E6	Grant St	53 F5
Drygate	58 C1	Eglinton Ct	57 H3	First Gdns	56 A4	Garvald St	59 F5	Granville St	53 F6
Duchray La	55 H5	Eglinton St	57 H3	Fisher Ct	58 D1	Gateside St	59 F2	Gray St	53 E5
Duchray St	55 H5	Elba La		Fitzroy La	53 E6	Gear Ter	59 F6	Great Dovehill	58 B2
Dudley Dr	52 A3	*off Gallowgate*	59 G3	Fitzroy Pl		General Terminus		Great George St	52 D3
Dudley La	52 A3	Elcho St	58 D2	*off Royal Ter*	53 E5	Quay	57 F2	Great Kelvin La	
Duke St	58 C1	Elderslie St	53 F5	Fleming St	59 F2	George Sq	58 A1	*off Glasgow St*	53 E4
Dumbarton Rd	52 A4	Eldon Ct		Flemington St	54 D3	George St	58 A1	Great Western Rd	53 E3
Dumbreck Av	56 A4	*off Caird Dr*	52 B4	Fleurs Av	56 B4	Gibson St		Great Western	
Dumbreck Ct	56 A5	Eldon St	53 E4	Fleurs Rd	56 B4	(Calton)	58 C2	Ter	52 C2
Dumbreck Path		Elgin St		Florence St	58 A3	Gibson St		Great Western	
off Dumbreck		*off Rowchester*		Forbes Dr	58 D3	(Hillhead)	53 E4	Ter La	52 C2
Av	56 A4	St	59 E3	Forbes St	58 D2	Gilbert St	52 C6	Green, The	58 C3
Dumbreck Pl	56 A5	Elie St	52 C4	Fordneuk St	59 E3	Gilmour Pl	58 A4	Greendyke St	58 B2
Dumbreck Rd	56 B5	Elizabeth St	56 C3	Ford Rd	52 D2	Girvan St	55 H5	Greenhead St	58 C4
Dumbreck Sq	56 A4	Ellesmere St	53 G2	Fordyce St	52 B4	Gladstone St	53 G4	Greenlodge Ter	
Dunard St	53 F2	Elliot Pl		Foremount		Glamis Rd	59 H4	*off Greenhead*	
Dunaskin St	52 C5	*off Finnieston*		Ter La	52 B3	Glasgow Br	57 H2	St	58 C4
Dunbeith Pl	52 D1	St	53 E6	Foresthall Cres	55 E3	Glasgow Cross	58 B2	Greenrig St	55 H3
Dunblane St	53 H5	Elliot St	57 E1	Foresthall Dr	55 E3	Glasgow Grn	58 B3	Green St	58 C3
Dunchattan Pl	58 D1	Elmbank Cres	53 G6	Forge Pl	55 F4	Glasgow Rd	58 D6	Gretna St	59 F4
Dunchattan St	58 D1	Elmbank La		Forge Retail Pk	59 F2	Glasgow St	53 E3	Grier Path	
Dunclutha St	59 F6	*off North St*	53 F6	Forge Shop Cen,		Glassford St	58 A1	*off Crail St*	59 H3
Dundashill	53 H4	Elmbank St	53 G6	The	59 G3	Glebe Ct	54 B6	Grierson La	
Dundas La	54 A6	Elmbank St La	53 G6	Forge St	55 F4	Glebe St	54 B5	*off Lomax St*	55 H6
Dundas St	54 A6	Elmfoot St	58 B6	Forrestfield St	55 E5	Glenapp St	57 F5	Grierson St	55 H6
Dundasvale Ct		Elmvale Row	54 C1	Forrest St	59 E3	Glenbarr St	54 D5	Grosvenor Cres	52 D3
off Maitland St	53 H5	Elmvale Row E		Forth St	57 F5	Glencairn Dr	56 D6	Grosvenor Cres La	
Dundasvale Rd		*off Elmvale Row*	54 C1	Fortrose St	52 B4	Glencairn Gdns	57 E6	*off Byres Rd*	52 D3
off Maitland St	53 H5	Elmvale Row W		Fotheringay La	56 D6	Glencairn La	57 F6	Grosvenor La	52 D3
Dundonald Rd	52 C2	*off Elmvale Row*	54 C1	Fotheringay Rd	56 D6	Glendale Pl	59 F2	Grosvenor Ter	52 D3
Dunearn St	53 F4	Elmvale St	54 C1	Foundry St	54 D2	Glendale St	59 F2	Grovepark Ct	53 G4
Dunkeld St	59 G4	Elphinstone Pl	56 C1	Fountainwell Av	54 B3	Glendarvel Gdns	54 B2	Grovepark Gdns	53 G4
Dunlop St	58 A2	Eltham St		Fountainwell Dr	54 B4	Glenfarg St	53 G4	Grovepark Pl	53 G3
Dunmore La		*off Bonhill St*	53 H3	Fountainwell Pl	54 B4	Glenisla St	59 H5	Grovepark St	53 G3
off Norfolk St	57 H3	Endrick St	54 B3	Fountainwell Rd	54 B4	Glenmavis St	53 H5	Gullane St	52 B5
Dunn St	59 E4	Errol Gdns	58 A4	Fountainwell Sq	54 C4	Glenpark Rd	59 F2	
Dunolly St	55 E5	Erskine Av	56 B4	Fountainwell Ter	54 C4	Glenpark St	59 F2	**H**
Dunragit St	59 G1	Esmond St	52 C5	Fourth Gdns	56 A4	Glenshee Ct	59 H5	Haggswood Av	56 C6
Dunrobin St	59 F2	Eton La	53 E4	Fox St	57 H2	Glenshee St	59 H4	Haghill Rd	59 G2
Dunsmuir St	56 B1	Ewing Pl	59 G3	Foyers Ter	55 E2	Glentrool Gdns	54 A2	Haig St	54 D2
Duntroon St	55 F6	Exchange Pl		Francis St	57 G4	Gloucester St	57 G3	Hallside Pl	58 A4
Durham St	56 D3	*off Buchanan*		Frankfield St	55 H4	Golfhill Dr	55 E6	Hamilton Av	56 D5
Dyce La	52 A4	St	58 A1	Franklin St	58 D5	Golfhill Ter		Hamilton Dr	53 E3
Dykemuir Pl		Exeter Dr	52 A4	Frazer St	59 E3	*off Firpark St*	54 D6	Hamiltonhill Cres	
off Dykemuir St	55 F2	Exeter La		French St	58 D5	Golspie St	52 A6	*off Hamiltonhill*	
Dykemuir Quad		*off Exeter Dr*	52 A4	Fruin Pl	54 A2	Goosedubbs		Rd	53 H2
off Dykemuir St	55 E2			Fruin St	54 A2	*off Stockwell St*	58 A2	Hamiltonhill Rd	53 H3
Dykemuir St	55 E2	**F**				Gorbals Cross	58 A3	Hamilton Pk Av	53 E3
		Fairbairn Path		**G**		Gorbals La		Handel Pl	58 A4
E		*off Ruby St*	59 E4	Gadie St	55 H6	*off Oxford St*	57 H4	Hannover Ct	54 A6
Eaglesham Ct		Fairbairn St	59 E4	Gadshill St	54 D5	Gorbals St	57 H4	Hanover St	58 A1
off Blackburn St	57 E2	Fairley St	56 B2	Gailes St	59 F4	Gordon La		Hanson Pk	54 D6
Eaglesham Pl	57 E2	Fairlie Pk Dr	52 A4	Gallowgate	58 B2	*off Mitchell St*	57 H1	Hanson St	54 D6
Eagle St	54 A4	Falfield St	57 G4	Gardner St	52 B4	Gordon St	57 H1	Harcourt Dr	55 F6
Earlston Av	54 D5	Falkland La	52 B3	Garfield St	59 E2	Gorstan Pl		Harley St	56 C3
Earlston Pl	54 D5	Falkland St	52 B3	Garmouth Ct	52 A6	*off Wyndford*		Harmony Ct	56 A1
Earnock St	55 H2	Farm Rd	56 B3	Garnet Ct		Rd	52 C1	Harmony Pl	56 A1
East Bath La		Farnell St	53 H4	*off New City*		Gough St	55 H6	Harmony Row	56 A1
off Sauchiehall		Fauldhouse St	58 B5	Rd	53 G5	Gourlay Path		Harmony Sq	
St	54 A6	Fergus Ct		Garnethill St	53 G5	*off Endrick St*	54 B3	*off Harmony*	
Eastburn Rd	55 F1	*off Fergus Dr*	53 E2	Garnet St	53 G5	Gourlay St	54 B3	Row	56 A1
East Campbell St	58 C2	Fergus Dr	53 E2	Garnock St	54 D4	Gourock St		Harrison Dr	
Eastcroft Ter	55 E2	Fergus La	53 F2	Garrioch Cres	52 D1	*off Eglinton St*	57 G4	*off Copland Rd*	56 B2
Eastercraigs	55 F6	Fernbank St	54 C1	Garrioch Dr	52 D1	Govan Cross		Harvey St	54 A4
Eastfield Rd	54 C2	Ferry Rd	52 B5	Garrioch Gate		*off Govan Rd*	52 A6	Harvie St	56 D2
Eastvale Pl	52 C6	Fielden Pl	59 E3	*off Garrioch Rd*	53 E1	Govan Cross Shop		Hastie St	52 D5
East Wellington		Fielden St	59 E3	Garriochmill Rd	53 E2	Cen	52 A6	Hathaway La	53 E1
St	59 H3	Findhorn St	55 H6	Garriochmill Way		Govanhill St	57 H6	Hathaway St	53 E1
East Whitby St	59 G4	Finlas St	54 B2	*off South*		Govan Rd	56 C2	Haugh Rd	52 D6
Eccles St	54 B2	Finlay Dr	59 E1	Woodside Rd	53 F3	Gower La		Havelock La	52 C4
off Carron St	54 C1	Finnart Sq	58 D5	Garrioch Quad	52 D1	*off North Gower*		Havelock St	52 C4
Edelweiss Ter		Finnart St	58 D5	Garrioch Rd	52 D2	St	56 D3	Hawthorn Quad	54 A1
off Gardner St	52 B4	Finnieston Quay	57 E1	Garscube Cross	53 H4	Gower St	56 C4	Hawthorn St	54 A1
Eden La	55 H5	Finnieston Sq		Garscube Rd	53 G3	Gower Ter	56 C3	Hayburn Ct	
Eden St	55 H5	*off Finnieston*		Gartferry St	54 D2	Grace St	57 F1	*off Hayburn St*	52 B4
Edgefauld Av	54 D3	St	53 E6	Garthland Dr	59 E1	Grafton Pl	54 A6	Hayburn Cres	52 A3
Edgefauld Dr	54 D2	Finnieston St	57 E1	Garth St		Graham Sq	58 D2	Hayburn Gate	52 A3
Edgefauld Pl	54 D1	Firhill Rd	53 G2	*off Glassford*		Graignestock Pl		Hayburn La	52 A3
Edgefauld Rd	54 D2	Firhill St	53 G2	St	58 A1	*off London Rd*	58 C3	Hayburn Pl	
Edgehill La	52 A2	Firpark Pl		Gartness St	59 F1	Graignestock St	58 C3	*off Hayburn St*	52 B4
Edinburgh Rd	59 H1	*off Firpark St*	54 D6	Gartons Rd	55 G1	Granby La	52 D3	Hayburn St	52 B5

Name	Ref		Name	Ref
Hayfield Ct	58 B4		Hughenden Rd	52 B2
Hayfield St	58 B4		Hughenden Ter	
Hayston Cres	53 H1		off Hughenden Rd	52 B2
Hayston St	53 H1		Hugo St	53 F1
Hazelwood Rd	56 C4		Hunter St	58 C2
Heddle Pl			Huntingdon Rd	54 C4
off Cadogan St	57 G1		Huntingdon Sq	54 C4
Helen St	56 A1		Huntly Gdns	52 C3
Helenvale Ct	59 H4		Huntly Rd	52 C3
Helenvale St	59 G4		Hutcheson St	58 A1
Henderson St	53 F3		Hutchinsontown Ct	58 A4
Herbertson St	57 H3		Hydepark St	57 F1
Herbert St	53 F3		Hyndland Av	52 B4
Heron St	58 D4		Hyndland Rd	52 B2
Herries Rd	56 C6		Hyndland St	52 C4
Herriet St	57 F5			
Hickman Ter	58 A6		**I**	
Hickory St	54 C1		Ibroxholm Av	56 B3
Highburgh Rd	52 C3		Ibroxholm Oval	56 B3
High Craighall Rd	53 H4		Ibroxholm Pl	
Highland La	52 C6		off Paisley Rd W	56 B3
High St	58 B2		Ibrox Ind Est	56 C2
Hillfoot St	59 E1		Ibrox St	56 C2
Hillhead Pl			Ibrox Ter	56 B2
off Bank St	53 E4		Ibrox Ter La	56 B2
Hillhead St	52 D4		India St	53 G6
Hillhouse St	55 E2		Ingleby Dr	59 E1
Hillkirk Pl			Inglefield St	57 H6
off Hillkirk St	54 C2		Inglis St	59 E2
Hillkirk St	54 C2		Ingram St	58 A1
Hillkirk St La			Inverleith St	59 H2
off Hillkirk St	54 D2		Invershin Dr	52 D1
Hillsborough Ter			Inverurie St	54 B3
off Bower St	53 E3		Iona St	56 B1
Hillside Gdns La			Irongray St	59 G1
off North Gardner St	52 B3		Irvine St	59 F5
Hill St	53 G5			
Hinshaw St	53 G3		**J**	
Hinshelwood Dr	56 A2		Jamaica St	57 H2
Hobart St	53 H2		James Morrison St	
Hobden St	55 E3		off St. Andrews Sq	58 B2
Hogarth Av	59 H1		James Nisbet St	54 C6
Hogarth Cres	59 H1		James St	58 C4
Hogarth Dr	59 H1		James Watt La	
Hogarth Gdns	59 H1		off James Watt St	57 G1
Hogganfield Ct	55 H4		James Watt St	57 G1
Hogganfield St	55 H4		Jamieson Ct	57 H6
Holland St	53 G6		Jamieson Path	
Hollybank St	55 E5		off Jamieson St	57 H6
Hollybrook Pl			Jamieson St	57 H6
off Hollybrook St	58 A6		Janefield St	59 F3
Hollybrook St	58 A6		Jane Pl	58 A4
Holly Dr	55 E3		Jardine St	
Holm St	57 G1		off Tillie St	53 F3
Holyrood Cres	53 F4		Jedburgh Gdns	
Holyrood Quad	53 F4		off Wilton St	53 F3
Holywell St	59 F3		Jessie St	58 B6
Hopefield Av	52 C1		Jocelyn Sq	58 A2
Hopehill Gdns	53 G3		John Knox La	
Hopehill Rd	53 G3		off Drygate	58 C1
Hope St	57 H1		John Knox St	58 C1
Hopetoun Ter	55 E3		John St	58 A1
Horne St			Julian Av	52 C2
off Hawthorn St	54 C1		Julian La	52 C2
Hornshill St	55 E2			
Horselethill Rd	52 C2		**K**	
Hospital St	58 A3		Karol Path	
Hotspur St	53 E1		off St. Peters St	53 G4
Houldsworth La			Kay St	54 D2
off Finnieston St	53 E6		Keir St	57 F5
Houldsworth St	53 E6		Keith Ct	52 C5
Houston Pl	57 F2		Keith St	52 C4
Houston St	57 F3		Kelbourne St	53 E2
Howard St	57 H2		Kellas St	56 A1
Howat St	52 A6		Kelty Pl	
Hughenden Dr	52 B2		off Bedford St	57 H3
Hughenden Gdns	52 A2		Kelvin Dr	52 D2
Hughenden La	52 B2			

Name	Ref		Name	Ref
Kelvingrove St	53 E6		Kinnear Rd	59 F5
Kelvinhaugh Gate	52 D6		Kinning Pk Ind Est	57 F3
Kelvinhaugh Pl			Kinning St	57 G3
off Kelvingrove St	52 D6		Kinnoul La	
Kelvinhaugh St	52 C6		off Downanside Rd	52 C3
Kelvinside Av	53 E2		Kintra St	56 B1
Kelvinside Dr	53 F2		Kintyre St	55 E5
Kelvinside Gdns	53 E2		Kirkcaldy Rd	56 D6
Kelvinside Gdns E	53 F3		Kirkhill Dr	53 E1
Kelvinside Gdns La	53 E2		Kirkhill Pl	
Kelvinside Ter S	53 E3		off Kirkhill Dr	52 D1
Kelvinside Ter W	53 E3		Kirkland St	53 F3
Kelvin Way	52 D5		Kirklee Circ	52 C2
Kempock St	59 G4		Kirklee Gdns	52 C1
Kemp St	54 C2		Kirklee Gdns La	52 D2
Kenmure St	57 F6		Kirklee Gate	52 D2
Kennedy Path			Kirklee Pl	52 D2
off St. Mungo Pl	54 B6		Kirklee Quad	52 D2
Kennedy St	54 B5		Kirklee Quad La	
Kennet St	55 E5		off Kirklee Quad	52 D2
Kennyhill Sq	55 F6		Kirklee Rd	52 C2
Kensington Gate			Kirklee Ter	52 C2
off Kensington Rd	52 C2		Kirklee Ter La	52 C2
Kensington Gate La	52 C2		Kirkmichael Av	
Kensington Rd	52 C2		off Blairatholl Av	52 A3
Kent Rd	53 E6		Kirkmichael Gdns	
Kent St	58 C2		off Blairatholl Av	52 A3
Keppochhill Dr	54 B3		Kirkpatrick St	59 E3
Keppochhill Pl	54 B4		Kirkwood St	56 C3
Keppochhill Rd	54 A3		Knowehead Gdns	57 E5
Keppochhill Way	54 B4		Knowehead Ter	57 E5
Keppoch St	54 B3		Kyle St	54 A5
Kerr Dr	58 D3			
Kerr Pl	58 D3		**L**	
Kerr St	58 D3		La Belle Allee	53 E5
Kerrydale St	59 F4		La Belle Pl	53 E5
Kersland La	52 D3		Laburnum Rd	56 C4
Kersland St	52 D3		La Crosse Ter	53 E3
Kessock Dr	53 H3		Ladywell St	58 C1
Kessock Pl	53 H3		Laidlaw St	57 G3
Kew Gdns			Laird Pl	58 D4
off Ruthven St	52 D3		Lambhill Quad	57 E3
Kew La	52 D3		Lambhill St	56 D3
Kew Ter	52 D3		Lanark St	58 B2
Kidston Pl	58 A4		Lancaster Cres La	52 C2
Kidston Ter	58 A4		Lancaster Ter	52 C2
Kilbarchan St			off Westbourne Gdns W	52 C2
off Bedford St	57 H3		Lancefield Quay	57 E1
Kilberry St	55 E5		Lancefield St	57 F1
Kilbirnie Pl	57 G4		Landressy Pl	58 C4
Kilbirnie St	57 G4		Landressy St	58 D4
Kilbride St	58 B6		Lane Gdns	
Kildonan Dr	52 A4		off North Gardner St	52 B3
Kildrostan St	57 F6		Langbank St	
Killearn St	53 H2		off Eglinton St	57 H3
Killermont St	54 A6		Langrig Rd	55 E2
Killiegrew Rd	56 D6		Langshot St	56 D3
Kilmair Pl	52 D1		Lansdowne Cres	53 F4
Kinbuck St	54 B2		Lansdowne Cres La	53 F4
Kingarth La	57 G6		Larbert St	53 H5
Kingarth St	57 G6		Larch Rd	56 B3
King George V Br	57 H2		Largs St	59 F1
Kingsborough Gdns	52 B3		Latherton Dr	52 D1
Kingsborough Gate			Latherton Pl	
off Prince Albert Rd	52 B3		off Latherton Dr	52 D1
Kingsborough La	52 B3		Laudedale La	52 B3
Kingsborough La E	52 B3		Lauderdale Gdns	52 B3
King's Br	58 B4		Laurel Pl	52 A3
Kings Cross	58 D1		Laurel St	52 A4
King's Dr	58 C4		Laurieston Rd	57 H4
Kingston Br	57 G2		Laverockhall St	54 D3
Kingston Ind Est	57 F3		Lawmoor Av	58 A5
Kingston St	57 G2		Lawmoor Pl	58 A6
King St	58 A2			
Kinloch St	59 G4			

Name	Ref
Lawmoor Rd	58 A5
Lawmoor St	58 A5
Lawrence St	52 C4
Lawrie St	52 B4
Law St	59 E3
Leadburn Rd	55 G2
Leader St	55 H5
Ledaig Pl	59 G1
Ledaig St	59 G1
Leicester Av	52 B1
Leith St	55 H6
Lendel Pl	
off Paisley Rd W	56 D3
Leny St	53 F2
Lenzie St	54 D1
Lenzie Ter	54 D1
Leslie Rd	57 E5
Leslie St	57 F5
Lettoch St	56 A1
Leven St	57 F5
Leyden Ct	53 E1
Leyden Gdns	53 E1
Leyden St	53 E1
Liberton St	55 H6
Lightburn Rd	59 G2
Lilybank Gdns	52 D4
Lilybank Gdns La	52 D4
Lilybank La	
off Lilybank Gdns	52 D4
Lilybank Ter	
off Great George St	52 D4
Lily St	59 F5
Lincluden Path	
off McCulloch St	57 F4
Linfern Rd	52 C3
Lismore Rd	52 B1
Lister St	54 B5
Little Dovehill	
off Gallowgate	58 B2
Little St	
off McIntyre St	57 F1
Lloyd St	55 E6
Lochgreen St	55 H3
Lochsloy Ct	54 B2
Lockhart St	55 H4
Logan St	58 B5
Lomax St	55 H6
Lomond St	53 H1
London Arc	
off London Rd	58 B2
London La	
off London Rd	58 B2
London Rd	58 B2
London Way	58 B2
Longford St	55 H6
Lorne St	56 D2
Lorraine Gdns	
off Kensington Rd	52 C2
Lorraine Gdns La	
off Westbourne Gdns La	52 C2
Lorraine Rd	
off Kensington Rd	52 C2
Lossie St	55 H5
Lothian Gdns	
off Wilton St	53 E3
Loudon Ter	
off Observatory Rd	52 D3
Lovat St	
off Borron St	54 A4
Lowther Ter	
off Redlands La	52 C2
Luath St	52 A6
Lumloch St	55 E2
Lumsden St	52 D6
Lymburn St	52 D5

Lyndhurst Gdns 53 F3
Lyndhurst Gdns
La 53 E2
Lynedoch Cres 53 F5
Lynedoch Cres La 53 F5
Lynedoch Pl 53 F5
Lynedoch St 53 F5
Lynedoch Ter 53 F5

M
McAlpine St 57 G1
McAslin Ct 54 B6
McAslin St 54 C6
Macbeth Pl 59 H4
Macbeth St 59 H4
McCulloch St 57 F4
Macduff Pl 59 H4
Macduff St 59 H4
McFarlane St 58 C2
McIntosh Ct 58 D1
McIntosh St 58 D1
McIntyre St 57 F1
McKechnie St 52 A6
Mackeith St 58 D4
Mackie St 54 A4
off Borron St
Mackinlay St 57 H4
Maclean Sq 56 D2
Maclean St 56 D2
Maclellan St 56 C3
Macleod St 54 C6
McNeil Gdns 58 B4
McNeil St 58 B4
McPhail St 58 C4
McPhater St 53 H5
Madras Pl 58 D5
Madras St 58 D5
Mafeking St 56 B2
Main St 58 D5
Mair St 57 E2
Maitland St 53 H5
Malloch St 53 E1
Malta Ter 57 H4
Maltbarns St 53 G3
Malvern Ct 59 E2
Manresa Pl 53 H4
Mansel St 54 D1
Mansfield St 52 C4
Mansion St 54 A1
Maple Rd 56 B4
March La
off Nithsdale
Dr 57 F6
Marchmont Ter
off Observatory
Rd 52 C3
March St 57 F6
Marine Cres 57 E2
Marine Gdns
off Mavisbank
Gdns 57 F2
Mariscat Rd 57 E6
Marlow St 57 E4
Marne St 59 F1
Martha St 54 A6
Martin St 58 D5
Mart St
off Bridgegate 58 A2
Marwick St 59 F1
Maryhill Rd 53 F3
Maryhill Shop
Cen 53 E1
Maryston Pl 55 H4
Maryston St 55 H4
Mary St 53 H4
Marywood Sq 57 F6
Masterton St 54 A3
Matilda Rd 57 E5
Mauchline St 57 G4
Maukinfauld Ct 59 H5
Mauldslie St 59 F4
Maule Dr 52 A4
Mavisbank Gdns 57 E2

Maxwell Av 57 E4
Maxwell Ct
off St. John's
Rd 57 E4
Maxwell Dr 56 C4
Maxwell Gdns 56 D4
Maxwell Gro 56 D4
Maxwell La
off Maxwell Dr 57 E4
Maxwell Oval 57 F4
Maxwell Pl 57 G5
Maxwell Rd 57 E4
Maxwell St 58 A2
Maxwell Ter 57 E4
Maxwelton Rd 55 H4
Meadowpark St 59 F1
Meadow Rd 52 A4
Meadowside St 52 A5
Megan Gate
off Megan St 58 D4
Megan St 58 D4
Melbourne St 58 D2
Meldrum Gdns 56 D6
Melfort Av 56 B4
Melrose Gdns 53 F3
Melrose St
off Queens Cres 53 F4
Melvaig Pl 52 D1
Melville St
off Brunswick
St 58 B2
Melville St 57 F5
Memel St 54 C1
Menzies Dr 55 E1
Menzies Pl 55 E1
Menzies Rd 55 E1
Merchant La 58 A2
Merkland Ct
off Vine St 52 B5
Merkland St 52 B4
Merrick Gdns 56 B3
Merrick Path
off Merrick
Gdns 56 B3
Merryland Pl 56 B1
Merryland St 56 B1
Methven St 59 H5
Metropole La
off Clyde St 58 A2
Middlesex Gdns 57 E2
Middlesex St 57 E3
Middleton St 56 C2
Midland St 57 H1
Midlock St 56 C3
Midton St 54 D3
Midwharf St 54 A4
Migvie Pl
off Wyndford
Rd 52 D1
Milan St 57 G5
Millarbank St 54 C2
Millburn St 54 D5
Mill Cres 58 D5
Millcroft Rd 58 D6
Millerfield Pl 59 F5
Millerfield Rd 59 F5
Millerston St 59 E2
Miller St 58 A1
Millroad Dr 58 C2
Millroad Gdns 58 D2
Millroad St 58 C2
Mill St 58 D5
Milnbank St 55 E6
Milnpark Gdns 56 D3
Milnpark St 57 E3
Milton St 54 A5
Minerva St 53 E6
Minerva Way 53 E6
Mingarry La
off Clouston
St 53 E2
Mingarry St 53 E2
Mireton St 53 H1

Mirrlees Dr 52 C2
Mirrlees La 52 C2
Mitchell La 57 H1
Mitchell St 57 H1
Moffat St 58 B4
Moir St 58 B2
Molendinar Gdns 55 H4
Molendinar St 58 B2
Mollinsburn St 54 C3
Monar Dr
off Monar St 53 H3
Monar Pl
off Monar St 53 H3
Monar St 53 H3
Monart Pl 53 F1
Moncur St 58 C2
Monkscroft Av 52 A3
Monkscroft Ct
off Crow Rd 52 A4
Monkscroft Gdns
off Monkscroft
Av 52 A3
Montague La 52 B2
Montague St 53 F4
Monteith Pl 58 C3
Monteith Row 58 C3
Monteith Row La
off Monteith Pl 58 C3
Montgomery St 59 E4
Montrose St 54 B6
Moodiesburn St 55 H4
Moore St
off Gallowgate 58 D2
Moray Pl 57 E6
Mordaunt St 59 E5
Morgan Ms 57 H5
Morningside St 55 H6
Morrin Path
off Crichton St 54 C2
Morrin Sq
off Collins St 54 C6
Morrin St 54 C2
Morrison Ct 57 H1
Morrison St 57 G2
Mosesfield St 54 D1
Mosque Av 58 A3
Mountainblue St 59 E3
Mount St 53 F3
Moy St
off Church St 52 C4
Muirhead St
off Purdon St 52 B4
Muirpark St 52 B4
Mull St 55 F4
Murano St 53 F2
Murdoch St
off Lenzie St 54 D1
Muslin St 58 D4
Myreside Pl 59 H2
Myreside St 59 H2

N
Naburn Gate 58 A4
Nairn St 52 D5
Nansen St 53 G3
Napier Dr 52 B6
Napier Pl 52 B6
Napier Rd 52 B6
Napiershall La 53 F4
Napiershall Pl
off Napiershall
St 53 F4
Napiershall St 53 F4
Napier Ter 52 B6
Nelson Mandela
Pl 54 A6
Nelson St 57 G2
Neptune St 56 B1
Nethan St 52 A6
Netherby Dr 56 D4
Netherfield St 59 G2
Newark Dr 56 D5
Newbank Gdns 59 H4

New City Rd 53 H5
Newhall St 58 C5
Newmill Rd 55 G1
Newton Pl 53 F5
Newton St
off Argyle St 53 G6
Newton Ter
off Sauchiehall
St 53 F6
Newton Ter La 53 F6
New Wynd 58 A2
Nicholas St 58 B1
Nicholson La
off Nicholson
St 57 H2
Nicholson St 57 H2
Niddrie Rd 57 F6
Niddrie Sq 57 F6
Nisbet St 59 H3
Nithsdale Dr 57 F6
Nithsdale Pl
off Nithsdale
Rd 57 F5
Nithsdale Rd 57 F6
Nithsdale St 57 F6
Nith St 55 H5
Norfolk Ct 57 H3
Norfolk La
off Norfolk St 57 H3
Norfolk St 58 A3
Norman St 58 D5
North Canal Bk 54 A4
North Canal Bk
St 54 A4
North Claremont
St off Royal
Ter 53 E5
North Ct
off St. Vincent
Pl 58 A1
North Ct La
off Buchanan
St 58 A1
Northcroft Rd 54 D2
North Dr 57 H1
North Frederick
St 54 A6
North Gardner St 52 B4
North Gower St 56 C3
North Hanover Pl
off North Hanover
St 54 A6
North Hanover
St 54 A6
Northpark St 53 F2
North Pl
off North St 53 F6
North Portland
St 58 B1
North St 53 F6
Northumberland
St 53 E2
North Wallace
St 54 B5
North Woodside
Rd 53 F3
Norval St 52 A4
Norwich Dr 52 B1
Novar Dr 52 A2
Nuneaton St 59 E5
Nuneaton St
Ind Est 59 E5
Nursery La 57 F6
Nursery St
off Pollokshaws
Rd 57 G5

O
Oakbank Ind Est 53 H3
Oakfield Av 53 E4
Oakfield La 53 E4
Oakley Ter 58 D1
Oak St 57 G1

Oatfield St 55 F2
Oban Ct
off Kelvinside
Gdns 53 E2
Oban Dr 53 E2
Oban La 53 E2
Observatory La
off Observatory
Rd 52 D3
Observatory Rd 52 C3
Ogilvie Pl 59 H4
Ogilvie St 59 H4
Old Dalmarnock
Rd 58 D4
Old Dumbarton
Rd 52 C5
Old Rutherglen
Rd 58 A4
Old Wynd 58 A2
Olive St 55 H2
Olympia St 58 D3
Onslow Dr 59 E1
Onslow Sq 59 E1
Oran Gdns 53 E1
Oran Gate 53 E1
Oran Pl 53 E2
Oran St 53 E1
Oregon Pl 58 A4
Orkney Pl
off Orkney St 56 A1
Orkney St 56 B1
Orr St 58 D3
Orton Pl 56 A2
Osborne St 58 A2
Oswald St 57 H2
Otago La 53 E4
Otago La N
off Otago St 53 E4
Otago St 53 E4
Overnewton Pl
off Kelvinhaugh
St 52 D6
Overnewton Sq
off Blackie St 52 D5
Overnewton St 52 D5
Overtown Pl 59 E3
Overtown St 59 E3
Oxford La 57 H3
Oxford St 57 H2

P
Pacific Dr 56 C2
Pacific Quay 56 D1
Paisley Rd 57 G2
Paisley Rd W 56 C3
Palermo St
off Atlas Rd 54 C2
Palmerston Pl
off Kelvinhaugh
St 52 D6
Panmure Cl 53 G2
Panmure St 53 G2
Park Av 53 F4
Park Circ 53 E5
Park Circ La 53 E5
Park Circ Pl 53 F5
Park Dr 53 E4
Park Gdns 53 E5
Park Gdns La 53 E5
Park Gate 53 E5
Parkgrove Ter 53 E5
Parkgrove Ter La
off Derby St 53 E5
Parkhead Cross 59 H3
Park Quad 53 E5
Park Rd 53 E4
Park St S 53 E5
Park Ter 53 E5
Park Ter E La 53 E5
Park Ter La 53 E5
Parnie St 58 A2
Parsonage Row 58 B1
Parsonage Sq 58 B1

Parson St 54 C6
Partick Br St 52 C4
Partickhill Av 52 B4
Partickhill Ct 52 B3
Partickhill Rd 52 B3
Paterson St 57 G3
Patna St 59 F5
Paton St 59 F1
Payne St 54 A4
Pearce La
  off Pearce St 52 A6
Pearce St 52 A6
Peathill St 54 A3
Peel La 52 B4
Peel St 52 B4
Pembroke St 53 F6
Penicuik St 59 H2
Percy St
  off Clifford St 56 D2
Perth St
  off Argyle St 57 F1
Petershill Ct 55 G2
Petershill Dr 55 F2
Petershill Pl 55 F2
Petershill Rd 54 D3
Phoenix Pk Ter
  off Corn St 53 H4
Phoenix Rd
  off Great Western Rd 53 G5
Piccadilly St 57 F1
Pine Pl 58 A4
Pinkston Dr 54 C4
Pinkston Rd 54 B3
Pitt St 57 G1
Plantation Pk Gdns
  off Clifford La 56 D3
Plantation Sq 57 E2
Plant St 59 G2
Playfair St 59 E5
Pointhouse Rd 57 E1
Pollokshaws Rd 57 G6
Pollokshields Sq
  off Glencairn Dr 57 F6
Polmadie Av 58 B6
Polmadie Ind Est 58 C6
Polmadie Rd 58 C5
Polwarth La 52 B2
Polwarth St 52 B3
Poplar Rd
  off Urrdale Rd 56 B3
Poplin St 58 D5
Port Dundas
  Ind Est 54 A4
Port Dundas Pl 54 A6
Port Dundas Rd 53 H5
Port Dundas
  Trd Centres 54 A4
Porter St 56 C3
Portman Pl
  off Cowan St 53 E4
Portman St 57 E3
Port St 53 F6
Portugal La
  off Bedford St 57 H3
Portugal St 57 H3
Possil Cross 54 A3
Possil Rd 53 H4
Powfoot St 59 H3
Preston Pl 57 H6
Preston St 57 H6
Prince Albert Rd 52 B3
Prince Edward St 57 H6
Prince's Dock 56 C1
Princes Gdns 52 B3
Princes Pl 52 C3
Princes Sq
  off Buchanan St 58 A1
Princes Ter 52 C3
Professors Sq 52 D4
Provanhill St 54 D5

Provanmill Pl
  off Provanmill Rd 55 H3
Provanmill Rd 55 H3
Provan Rd 55 G5
Purdon St 52 B4

Q
Quarrybrae St 59 H3
Quarrywood Av 55 G2
Quarrywood Rd 55 H2
Queen Elizabeth Gdns 58 A4
Queen Elizabeth Sq 58 B4
Queen Margaret Ct
  off Fergus Dr 53 E2
Queen Margaret Dr 52 D3
Queen Margaret Rd 53 E2
Queen Mary St 58 D4
Queensborough Gdns 52 A2
Queens Cres 53 F4
Queens Dr 57 F6
Queensferry St 58 C6
Queens Gdns
  off Victoria Cres Rd 52 C3
Queens Gate La
  off Victoria Cres Rd 52 C3
Queenslie St 55 H4
Queens Pl 52 C3
Queen Sq 57 F6
Queen St 58 A1

R
Radnor St
  off Argyle St 52 D6
Raeberry St 53 F3
Rafford St 56 A1
Raglan St 53 G4
Rathlin St 52 A6
Ratho Dr 54 C1
Ravel Row 59 H3
Ravelston St 59 H2
Redan St 58 D3
Redford St 55 H6
Redlands La 52 C2
Redlands Rd 52 C2
Redlands Ter
  off Julian Av 52 C2
Redlands Ter La 52 C2
Redmoss St 53 H1
Rednock St 54 A2
Red Rd 55 F2
Red Rd Ct 55 F3
Redwood Dr 55 E3
Regent Moray St 52 D5
Regent Pk Sq 57 F6
Reidhouse St 54 D2
Reid Pl 58 D4
Reid St 58 D5
Reidvale St 58 D2
Renfield La
  off Hope St 57 H1
Renfield St 57 H1
Renfrew Ct 53 H6
Renfrew La
  off Hope St 53 H6
Renfrew St 53 H6
Renton St 54 A5
Rhymer St 54 C5
Rhynie Dr 56 B3
Riccarton St 58 A6
Richard St
  off Cadzow St 57 G1
Richmond St 58 B1
Rimsdale St 59 E3
Ringford St 54 D3

Ritchie St 57 G4
Riverview Dr 57 G2
Riverview Gdns 57 G2
Riverview Pl 57 G2
Robert Dr 52 A6
Roberton Av 56 C6
Robertson La 57 G1
Robertson St 57 H1
Robert St 52 A6
Robson Gro 57 H5
Rockbank Pl 59 E3
Rockbank St 59 E3
Rockcliffe St 58 D5
Rockfield Pl 55 G1
Rockfield Rd 55 G1
Rock St 53 H3
Rodney St 53 H4
Roebank St 55 F6
Rogart St 58 D3
Rona St 55 F4
Ropework La
  off Clyde St 58 A2
Roseberry St 58 C5
Rosemount Cres 54 D6
Rosemount St 54 D5
Rose St 53 H6
Rosevale St 52 A4
Roslea Dr 59 E1
Rosneath St 52 A6
Rosslyn Ter 52 C2
Ross St 58 B2
Rosyth Rd 58 C6
Rosyth St 58 C6
Rottenrow 54 B6
Rottenrow E 58 B1
Rowallan Gdns 52 A3
Rowallan La E 52 A3
Rowan Gdns 56 B4
Rowan Rd 56 B4
Rowchester St 59 E3
Roxburgh La
  off Saltoun St 52 D3
Roxburgh St 52 D3
Royal Bk Pl
  off Buchanan St 58 A1
Royal Cres 53 E6
Royal Ex Bldgs
  off Royal Ex Sq 58 A1
Royal Ex Ct
  off Queen St 58 A1
Royal Ex Sq 58 A1
Royal Ter 53 E5
Royal Ter La 53 E5
Roystonhill 54 D5
Roystonhill Pl 54 D5
Royston Rd 54 C5
Royston Sq 54 C5
Roy St 54 B3
Ruby St 59 E4
Ruchill Pl
  off Ruchill St 53 F1
Ruchill St 53 E1
Rumford St 58 D5
Rupert St 53 F4
Rushyhill St 55 E2
Ruskin La 53 E3
Ruskin Pl 53 E3
Ruskin Ter 53 E3
Russell St
  off Vine St 52 B4
Rutherglen Br 58 D5
Rutherglen Rd 58 B5
Ruthven La 52 D3
Ruthven St 52 D3
Rutland Ct
  off Govan Rd 57 E2
Rutland Cres 57 E2
Rutland Pl 57 E2
Ryebank Rd 55 G1
Rye Cres 55 F1
Ryefield Rd 55 F1
Ryehill Pl 55 G1

Ryehill Rd 55 G1
Ryemount Rd 55 G1
Rye Rd 55 F1
Ryeside Rd 55 F1

S
St. Andrews Cres 57 E4
St. Andrews Cross 57 G5
St. Andrews Dr 57 E4
St. Andrews La
  off Gallowgate 58 B2
St. Andrews Rd 57 F4
St. Andrews Sq 58 B2
St. Andrews St 58 B2
St. Clair St
  off North Woodside Rd 53 F4
St. Enoch Shop Cen 58 A2
St. Enoch Sq 57 H2
St. Francis Rigg 58 A4
St. Georges Pl
  off St. Georges Rd 53 G5
St. Georges Rd 53 G4
St. James Rd 54 B6
St. John's Ct 57 E4
St. John's Quad 57 E4
St. John's Rd 57 E5
St. Joseph's Ct 54 D5
St. Joseph's Pl 54 D5
St. Joseph's Vw 54 D5
St. Luke's Pl 58 A3
St. Luke's Ter 58 A3
St. Margarets Pl
  off Bridgegate 58 A2
St. Marnock St 59 E3
St. Marys La
  off West Nile St 57 H1
St. Michael's Ct 59 G3
St. Michael's La
  off St. Michael's La 59 G3
St. Michael's La 59 G3
St. Monance St 54 D1
St. Mungo Av 54 A6
St. Mungo Pl 54 B6
St. Ninian Ter 58 A3
  off Ballater St 58 A3
St. Peters La
  off Blythswood St 57 G1
St. Peter's Path
  off Braid St 53 G4
St. Peters St 53 G4
St. Rollox Brae 54 C4
St. Valentine Ter 58 B4
St. Vincent Cres 52 D6
St. Vincent Cres La 52 D6
St. Vincent La
  off Hope St 53 G6
St. Vincent Pl 58 A1
St. Vincent St 53 G6
St. Vincent Ter 53 F6
Salamanca St 59 H3
Salisbury Pl 57 H4
Salisbury St 57 H4
Salkeld St 57 H4
Salmona St 53 H2
Saltmarket 58 A2
Saltmarket Pl
  off Bridgegate 58 A2
Saltoun Gdns
  off Roxburgh St 52 D3
Saltoun La 52 D3
Saltoun St 52 C3
Sanda St 53 E2
Sandfield St 53 E1
Sandiefield Rd 58 A4
Sandmill St 55 E5
Sandringham La
  off Kersland St 52 D3

Sandyford Pl
  off Sauchiehall St 53 F6
Sandyford Pl La 53 E6
Sandyford St 52 C6
Sandy La
  off Crawford St 52 A4
Sandy Rd 52 A5
Sannox Gdns 55 F6
Saracen Head La
  off Gallowgate 58 C2
Saracen St 54 A3
Sardinia La 52 D3
Sardinia Ter
  off Cecil St 52 D3
Sauchiehall La
  off Sauchiehall St 53 G6
Sauchiehall St 53 G6
Savoy St 58 D4
Sawmillfield St 53 H4
Schipka Pas
  off Gallowgate 58 B2
Scone St 54 A3
Scotland St 57 F3
Scotland St W 57 E3
Scotsburn Rd 55 G2
Scotstoun Mill Rd
  off Partick Br St 52 C5
Scott St 53 G6
Seagrove St 59 H2
Seamore St 53 F4
Seath St 58 A6
Seaward La 57 E2
Seaward Pl 57 E4
Seaward St 57 F3
Second Gdns 56 A4
Seton Ter 58 D1
Shaftesbury St 53 F6
Shakespeare St 53 E1
Shamrock St 53 G5
Shanks St 53 E1
Shannon St 53 F1
Shawfield Dr 58 C6
Shawfield Ind Est 58 D6
Shawfield Rd 58 D5
Shearer St
  off Paisley Rd 57 F2
Shelley Ct 52 A1
Sheppard St
  off Cowlairs Rd 54 C2
Sherbrooke Av 56 C5
Sherbrooke Dr 56 C4
Sherbrooke Gdns 56 C5
Shettleston Rd 59 G2
Shields Rd 57 F3
Shipbank La
  off Clyde St 58 A2
Shore St 58 D6
Shortridge St 53 E1
Shuna Gdns 53 F1
Shuna Pl 53 E1
Shuttle La
  off George St 58 B1
Shuttle St 58 B1
Sidland Rd 55 G1
Siemens Pl 55 F4
Siemens St 55 F4
Silverdale St 59 G4
Silverfir Ct 58 B5
Silverfir Pl 58 B5
Silverfir St 58 B5
Silvergrove St 58 C3
Simpson St 53 F3
Skene Rd 56 B3
Slatefield Ct
  off Slatefield St 59 E2
Slatefield St 59 E2
Sloy St 54 B2
Snowdon Pl
  off Benthall St 58 B4

GLASGOW

Snowdon St
  off Benthall St 58 B4
Society St 59 F3
Solway St 58 D6
Somerset Pl 53 F5
Somerset Pl Ms 53 F5
Sorby St 59 H3
Sorn St 59 F5
South Annandale
  St 57 H6
Southbank St 59 H3
Southcroft St 56 B1
South Ex Ct
  off Queen St 58 A1
South Frederick
  St 58 A1
Southloch Gdns 54 D3
Southloch St 54 D3
Southmuir Pl 52 D1
Southpark Av 52 D4
Southpark La 53 E4
Southpark Ter
  off Southpark
  Av 53 E4
South Portland
  St 57 H3
Southside Cres 57 H4
South Woodside
  Rd 53 F3
Spiers Wf 53 H4
Spoutmouth
  off Gallowgate 58 B2
Springbank St 53 F2
Springburn Rd 54 C4
Springburn Shop
  Cen 54 D2
Springburn Way 54 C2
Springfield Ct
  off Buchanan
  St 58 A1
Springfield Quay 57 F2
Springfield Rd 59 F5
Springkell Av 56 C5
Springkell Dr 56 B6
Springkell Gdns 56 C6
Springkell Gate 56 D6
Spring La
  off Lawmoor
  St 58 A5
Springvale Ter 54 C2
Spring Wynd 58 A4
Spruce St 54 B1
Staffa St 55 F6
Stafford St 54 B5
Stag St 56 B1
Stair St 53 F2
Stamford Pl 59 F3
Stamford Rd 59 F3
Stamford St 59 F3
Stanley St 57 E3
Stanley St La 57 E3
Steel St 58 B2
Stevenson St 58 C2
Stewart St 53 H5
Stewartville St 52 B4
Stirlingfauld Pl 57 H3
Stirling Rd 54 B6
Stobcross Rd 52 D6
Stobcross St 57 F1
Stobcross Wynd 52 C6
Stockwell Pl 58 A2
Stockwell St 58 A2
Stonyhurst St 53 H2
Stratford St 52 D1
Strathbran St 59 H4
Strathclyde St 59 E6
Striven Gdns 53 F3
Stroma St 55 F4
Stromness St 57 G4
Stronend St 53 H1
Stronsay St 55 F4
Suffolk St
  off Kent St 58 C2
Summerfield St 59 F6

Summer St 58 D3
Summertown Rd 56 B1
Sunnybank St 59 F5
Sunnylaw St 53 H2
Surrey St 57 H4
Sussex St 57 E3
Sutherland Av 56 B5
Sutherland La 52 C4
Swanston St 59 E6
Swan St 54 A5
Sword St 58 D2
Sydenham La
  off Crown Rd S 52 B3
Sydenham Rd 52 C3
Sydney St 58 C2
Syriam Pl
  off Syriam St 54 D2
Syriam St 54 D2

T
Tamworth St
  off Rimsdale St 59 E3
Tannock St 53 H2
Taransay St 52 A6
Taylor Pl 54 B6
Taylor St 58 B1
Telephone La 52 C3
Templetons
  Business Cen 58 C3
Templeton St 58 C3
Terregles Av 56 B6
Terregles Cres 56 B6
Terregles Dr 56 C6
Teviot St 52 C6
Teviot Ter
  off Sanda St 53 E2
Tharsis St 54 D5
Third Gdns 56 A4
Thistle St 58 A3
Thistle Ter 58 A4
Thomson St 59 E2
Thornbank St 52 C5
Thornbridge Av
  off Balcarres
  Av 52 C1
Thorncliffe Gdns 57 E6
Thorncliffe La 57 E6
Thornhill Path
  off Crail St 59 H4
Thornwood Av 52 A4
Thornwood Gdns 52 A4
Thornwood Pl 52 A3
Thurso St 52 C3
Tibbermore Rd 52 A3
Tillie St 53 F3
Tiree St 55 G4
Tobago Pl 58 D3
Tobago St 58 C3
Todd St 59 G1
Toll Ct 57 E2
Tollcross Rd 59 H3
Tontine La 58 B2
Torness St 52 C4
Torrance St 54 D2
Torr Gdns 54 B2
Torridon Av 56 B5
Torridon Path
  off Dumbreck
  Av 56 A5
Torrisdale St 57 F6
Torr Pl 54 B2
Torr St 54 B2
Torryburn Rd 55 G2
Toryglen St 58 B6
Tower St 57 E3
Townmill Rd 54 D6
Townsend St 54 A5
Tradeston St 57 G3
Trafalgar St 58 D5
Trongate 58 A2
Troon St 59 F5
Trossachs Ct
  off Trossachs
  St 53 G3

Trossachs St 53 G3
Tullis Ct 58 C4
Tullis St 58 C4
Tunnel St 57 E1
Tureen St 58 D2
Turnberry Av
  off Turnberry
  Rd 52 B3
Turnberry Rd 52 A3
Turnbull St 58 B2
Turner Rd 54 D4
Turnlaw St 58 B4
Turriff St 57 H4
Tweed Cres 55 H5
Tyndrum St 54 A5

U
Union Pl
  off Gordon St 57 H1
Union St 57 H1
Unity Pl 53 G4
University Av 52 D4
University Gdns 52 D4
University of
  Glasgow 52 D4
University Pl 52 D4
Urrdale Rd 56 B3

V
Valleyfield St
  off Ayr St 54 C3
Vasart Pl 53 F1
Vennard Gdns 57 E6
Vermont St 57 E3
Vicarfield Pl
  off Vicarfield
  St 56 B1
Vicarfield St 56 B1
Victoria Br 58 A2
Victoria Circ 52 C3
Victoria Cres
  off Dowanside
  Rd 52 C3
Victoria Cres La 52 C3
Victoria Cres Pl
  off Bowmont
  Ter 52 C3
Victoria Cres Rd 52 C3
Victoria Cross 57 G6
Viewfield La 53 E4
Viewpark Av 55 F6
Vine St 52 B4
Vinicombe La 52 D3
Vinicombe St 52 D3
Vintner St 54 A4
Virginia Bldgs
  off Virginia St 58 A1
Virginia Ct
  off Virginia St 58 A1
Virginia Pl 58 A1
Virginia St 58 A1
Vulcan St
  off Springburn
  Way 54 C2

W
Waddell Ct 58 B3
Waddell St 58 B4
Walker Ct 52 B5
Walker St 52 B5
Walkinshaw St 59 E4
Wallace St 57 G2
Wallacewell Cres 55 F1
Wallacewell Pl 55 F1
Wallacewell Rd 55 F1
Walls St 58 B1
Walmer Cres 56 C2
Walnut Cres 54 B1
Walnut Pl 54 B1
Walnut Rd 54 B1
Walter St 59 F1
Wanlock St 52 A6
Wardhill Rd 55 F1
Wardrop St 52 A6

Warnock St 54 C6
Warriston Cres 55 H6
Warriston St 55 H6
Warroch St 57 F1
Washington St 57 G1
Waterloo La
  off Waterloo
  St 57 H1
Waterloo St 57 G1
Water Row 52 A6
Waterside Pl 58 B4
Waterside St 58 B4
Watson St 58 B2
Watt St 57 F2
Waverley Ter
  off Whitevale
  St 59 E2
Weaver St 58 B1
Webster St 59 E5
Wellcroft Pl 57 H4
Wellfield St 54 D2
Wellington La 57 G1
Wellington St 57 H1
Wellpark St 58 C1
Westbank Ct 53 E4
Westbank La 53 E4
Westbank Quad 53 E4
Westbourne
  Gdns La 52 C2
Westbourne
  Gdns N 52 C2
Westbourne
  Gdns S 52 C2
Westbourne
  Gdns W 52 C2
Westbourne Rd 52 B2
Westbourne Ter La
  off Westbourne
  Rd 52 B2
West Campbell
  St 57 G1
West End Pk St 53 F5
Wester Common
  Dr 53 G1
Wester Common
  Rd 53 G2
Wester Common
  Ter 53 H2
Westercraigs 58 D1
Westercraigs Ct
  off Westercraigs 58 D1
West George La
  off Pitt St 53 G6
West George St 53 G6
West Graham St 53 G5
West Greenhill Pl 53 E6
Westminster Gdns
  off Kersland St 52 D3
Westminster Ter
  off Royal Ter 53 E6
Westmoreland St 57 G6
Westmuir St 59 H3
West Nile St 57 H1
West Princes St 53 F4
West Regent La
  off Hope St 53 H6
West Regent St 53 G6
Westside Gdns 52 B4
West St 57 G3
West Whitby St 59 G4
Whitefield Rd 56 C3
Whitehall St 57 F1
Whitehill Ct 59 E1
Whitehill Gdns 59 E1
Whitehill Pl 59 E1
Whitehill St 59 E1
Whitehill St La 59 E1
White St 52 B4
Whitevale St 59 E2
Whittingehame
  Gdns 52 A1
Whitworth Gate 53 G1
Williamson St 59 G4
William St 53 F6

Willowbank Cres
  off Woodlands
  Rd 53 F4
Willowbank St 53 F4
Wilson St 58 A1
Wilton Cres 53 F3
Wilton Cres La 53 F3
Wilton Dr 53 F3
Wilton Gdns 53 F3
Wilton St 53 E3
Windmillcroft
  Quay 57 G2
Windsor St 53 G4
Windsor Ter 53 G4
Winifred St 55 H2
Winning Row 59 H3
Winton Dr 52 C1
Winton La 52 C1
Wishart St 58 C1
Woddrop St 59 F6
Wolseley St 58 B5
Woodhall St 59 F6
Woodlands Dr 53 F4
Woodlands Gate 53 F5
Woodlands Rd 53 F4
Woodlands Ter 53 E5
Woodrow Circ 56 C4
Woodrow Pl 56 C4
Woodrow Rd 56 D4
Woodside Cres 53 F5
Woodside Pl 53 F5
Woodside Pl La 53 F5
Woodside Ter 53 F5
Woodside Ter La 53 F5
Wood St 55 F6
Woodville Pk 56 B2
Woodville St 56 B2
Wyndford Dr 52 D1
Wyndford Pl
  off Wyndford
  Rd 52 D1
Wyndford Rd 52 C1
Wyndham Ct
  off Wyndham
  St 52 D2
Wyndham St 52 D2
Wyper Pl 59 E2

Y
Yarrow Gdns 53 F3
Yarrow Gdns La
  off Yarrow
  Gdns 53 F3
Yate Gro 59 F3
Yate Rd 59 F3
Yate St 59 F3
Yew Dr 55 E3
Yorkhill Par 52 C5
Yorkhill Quay 52 B6
Yorkhill St 52 D6
York St 57 G2
Young Ter 55 E2

Z
Zena Cres 55 G2
Zena Pl 55 H2
Zena St 55 H2

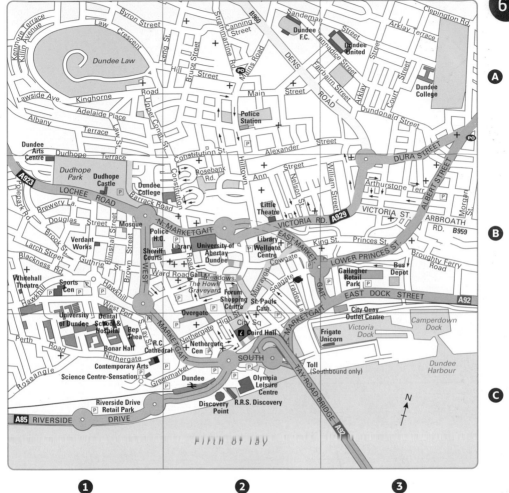

0 ____ 400 yds
0 ____ 400m

Tourist Information Centre: 21 Castle Street
Tel: 01382 527527

Adelaide Place	A1	Clepington Road	A3	Kenmore Terrace	A1	Polepark Road	B1
Albany Terrace	A1	Constitution Road	B2	Killin Avenue	A1	Princes Street	B3
Albert Street	B3	Constitution Street	A2	Kinghorne Road	A1	Riverside Drive	C1
Alexander Street	A2	Court Street	A3	King Street	B2	Roseangle	C1
Ann Street	B2	Cowgate Street	B2	Larch Street	B1	Rosebank Road	B2
Arbroath Road	B3	Dens Road	A2	Law Crescent	A1	Seagate	B2
Arklay Street	A3	Douglas Street	B1	Lawside Avenue	A1	South Marketgait	C2
Arklay Terrace	A3	Dudhope Street	A1	Law Street	A1	South Tay Street	C1
Arthurstone Terrace	B3	Dudhope Terrace	A3	Leng Street	A1	Strathmartine Road	A2
Barrack Road	B1	Dundonald Street	A3	Lochee Road	B1	Tannadice Street	A2
Blackness Road	B1	Dura Street	B3	Lower Princes Street	B3	Tay Road Bridge	C2
Blinshall Street	B1	East Dock Street	B3	Mains Road	A2	Trades Lane	B2
Brewery Lane	B1	East Marketgait	B2	Main Street	A2	Upper Constitution Street	A1
Brook Street	B1	Fairbairn Street	A2	Meadowside	B2	Victoria Road	B2
Broughty Ferry Road	B3	Greenmarket	C2	Morgan Street	B3	Victoria Street	B3
Brown Street	B1	Guthrie Street	B1	Murraygate	B2	Ward Road	B1
Bruce Street	A1	Hawkhill	B1	Nelson Street	B2	West Marketgait	B1
Byron Street	A1	High Street	C2	Nethergate	C1	West Port	B1
Canning Street	A2	Hill Street	A2	North Marketgait	B1	William Street	B3
City Square	C2	Hilltown	A2	Perth Road	C1		

DUNDEE

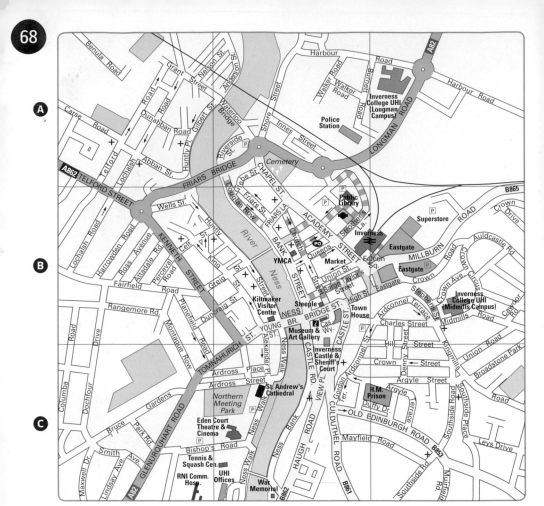

A

B

C

1 2 3

0 ——————— 300 yds
0 ——————— 300m

Tourist Information Centre: Castle Wynd
Tel: 0845 22 55 121

Abban Street	A1	Chapel Street	A2	Greig Street	B1	Old Edinburgh Road	C2
Academy Street	B2	Charles Street	B3	Harbour Road	A2	Park Road	C1
Alexander Place	B2	Church Street	B2	Harrowden Road	B1	Perceval Road	B1
Anderson Street	A2	Columba Road	C1	Haugh Road	C2	Planefield Road	B1
Ardconnel Street	C2	Crown Avenue	B3	High Street	B2	Queensgate	B2
Ardconnel Terrace	B3	Crown Circus	B3	Hill Street	B3	Rangemore Road	B1
Ardross Place	C2	Crown Drive	B3	Hontly Place	A1	Riverside Street	A2
Ardross Street	C2	Crown Road	B3	Huntly Street	B1	Ross Avenue	B1
Argyle Street	C3	Crown Street	C3	Innes Street	A2	Shore Street	A2
Argyle Terrace	C3	Culduthel Road	C2	Kenneth Street	B1	Smith Avenue	C1
Attadale Road	B1	Denny Street	C3	Kingsmills Road	B3	Southside Place	C3
Auldcastle Road	B3	Dochfour Drive	C1	King Street	B1	Southside Road	C3
Bank Street	B2	Douglas Row	A2	Leys Drive	C3	Stephens Street	B3
Baron Taylor's Street	B2	Duffy Drive	C2	Lindsay Avenue	C1	Strother's Lane	B2
Benula Road	A1	Duncraig Street	B1	Lochalsh Road	A1	Telford Road	A1
Bishop's Road	C1	Eastgate	B3	Longman Road	A3	Telford Street	A1
Bridge Street	B2	Fairfield Road	B1	Maxwell Drive	C1	Tomnahurich Street	C1
Broadstone Park	C3	Falcon Square	B2	Mayfield Road	C2	Union Road	B3
Bruce Gardens	C1	Friars Bridge	A1	Midmills Road	B3	Union Street	B2
Burnett Road	A3	Friars Lane	B2	Millburn Road	B3	View Place	C2
Carse Road	A1	Friars Street	B2	Montague Row	B1	Walker Road	A2
Castle Road	B2	Gilbert Street	A1	Muirfield Road	C3	Waterloo Bridge	A2
Castle Street	B2	Glebe Street	A2	Nelson Street	A1	Wells Street	B1
Castle Wynd	B2	Glen Urquhart Road	C1	Ness Bank	C2	Young Street	B2
Cawdor Road	B3	Gordon Terrace	C2	Ness Bridge	B2		
Celt Street	B1	Grant Street	A1	Ness Walk	C2		

Tourist Information Centre: Lower City Mills, West Mill Street
Tel: 01738 450600

PERTH

Aberdeen to Kirkwall
6 hrs - 7 hrs 15 mins
All Year
North Link Ferries
0845 6000 449
www.northlinkferries.co.uk

Aberdeen to Lerwick
12 hrs 30 mins
All Year
North Link Ferries
0845 6000 449
www.northlinkferries.co.uk

Ardrossan to Brodick
55 mins
All Year
Caledonian MacBrayne
08000 66 5000
www.calmac.co.uk

Barra to Eriskay
40 mins
All Year
Caledonian MacBrayne
08000 66 5000
www.calmac.co.uk

Belmont to Gutcher
10 mins
All Year
Shetland Islands Council
01806 244219
www.shetland.gov.uk/ferries/

Belmont to Oddsta
30 mins
All Year
Shetland Islands Council
01806 244219
www.shetland.gov.uk/ferries/

Cairnryan to Larne
1 hr - 1hr 45 mins
All Year
P&O Irish Sea
0870 24 24 777
www.poirishsea.com

Castlebay to Lochboisdale
1 hr 50 mins
All Year
Caledonian MacBrayne
08000 66 5000
www.calmac.co.uk

Claonaig to Lochranza
30 mins
Summer Only
Caledonian MacBrayne
08000 66 5000
www.calmac.co.uk

Colintraive to Rhubodach
5 mins
All Year
Caledonian MacBrayne
08000 66 5000
www.calmac.co.uk

Coll to Tiree
55 mins - 1 hr
All Year
Caledonian MacBrayne
08000 66 5000
www.calmac.co.uk

Colonsay to Port Askaig
1 hr 20 mins
Summer Only
Caledonian MacBrayne
08000 66 5000
www.calmac.co.uk

Cromarty to Nigg
5 mins
Summer Only
Cromarty Ferry Company
01381 610269

Eday to Sanday
20 mins
All Year
Orkney Ferries
01856 872044
www.orkneyferries.co.uk

Eday to Stronsay
35 mins
All Year
Orkney Ferries
01856 872044
www.orkneyferries.co.uk

Egilsay to Rousay
20 mins
All Year
Orkney Ferries
01856 872044
www.orkneyferries.co.uk

Egilsay to Wyre
20 mins
All Year
Orkney Ferries
01856 872044
www.orkneyferries.co.uk

Feolin to Port Askaig
5 mins
All Year
Argyll & Bute Council
01496 840681

Gill's Bay to St. Margaret's Hope
1 hr
All Year
Pentland Ferries
01856 831226
www.pentlandferries.co.uk

Glenelg to Kylerhea
5 mins
Summer Only
Skye Ferry
01599 522273
www.skyeferry.co.uk

Gourock to Dunoon
20 mins
All Year
Caledonian MacBrayne
08000 66 5000
www.calmac.co.uk

Gourock to Dunoon
20 mins
All Year
Western Ferries
01369 704452
www.western-ferries.co.uk

Gutcher to Oddsta
25 mins
All Year
Shetland Islands Council
01806 244219
www.shetland.gov.uk/ferries/

Houton to Flotta
30 mins
All Year
Orkney Ferries
01856 872044
www.orkneyferries.co.uk

Houton to Lyness
35 mins
All Year
Orkney Ferries
01856 872044
www.orkneyferries.co.uk

Kennacraig to Port Askaig
2 hrs 5 mins
All Year
Caledonian MacBrayne
08000 66 5000
www.calmac.co.uk

Kennacraig to Port Ellen
2 hrs 20 mins
All Year
Caledonian MacBrayne
08000 66 5000
www.calmac.co.uk

Kirkwall to Eday
1 hr 15 mins
All Year
Orkney Ferries
01856 872044
www.orkneyferries.co.uk

Kirkwall to North Ronaldsay
3 hrs
All Year
Orkney Ferries
01856 872044
www.orkneyferries.co.uk

Kirkwall to Papa Westray
1 hr 50 mins
All Year
Orkney Ferries
01856 872044
www.orkneyferries.co.uk

Kirkwall to Sanday
1 hr 25 mins
All Year
Orkney Ferries
01856 872044
www.orkneyferries.co.uk

Kirkwall to Shapinsay
25 mins
All Year
Orkney Ferries
01856 872044
www.orkneyferries.co.uk

Kirkwall to Stronsay
1 hr 35 mins
All Year
Orkney Ferries
01856 872044
www.orkneyferries.co.uk

Kirkwall to Westray
1 hr 25 mins
All Year
Orkney Ferries
01856 872044
www.orkneyferries.co.uk

Largs to Cumbrae Slip
10 mins
All Year
Caledonian MacBrayne
08000 66 5000
www.calmac.co.uk

Laxo to Symbister
30 mins
All Year
Shetland Islands Council
01806 244219
www.shetland.gov.uk/ferries/

Lerwick to Bressay
5 mins
All Year
Shetland Islands Council
01806 244219
www.shetland.gov.uk/ferries/

Lerwick to Kirkwall
5 hrs 30 mins - 7 hrs 45 mins
All Year
North Link Ferries
0845 6000 449
www.northlinkferries.co.uk

Lerwick to Skerries
2 hrs 30 mins
All Year
Shetland Islands Council
01806 244219
www.shetland.gov.uk/ferries/

Leverburgh to Berneray
1 hr
All Year
Caledonian MacBrayne
08000 66 5000
www.calmac.co.uk

Lochaline to Fishnish
15 mins
All Year
Caledonian MacBrayne
08000 66 5000
www.calmac.co.uk

Longhope to Flotta
30 mins
All Year
Orkney Ferries
01856 872044
www.orkneyferries.co.uk

Longhope to Lyness
30 mins
All Year
Orkney Ferries
01856 872044
www.orkneyferries.co.uk

Luing to Seil
5 mins
All Year
Oban Tourist Information Centre
01631 563122

Lyness to Flotta
30 mins
All Year
Orkney Ferries
01856 872044
www.orkneyferries.co.uk

Mallaig to Armadale
30 mins
All Year
Caledonian MacBrayne
08000 66 5000
www.calmac.co.uk

Oban to Castlebay
4 hrs 50 mins
All Year
Caledonian MacBrayne
08000 66 5000
www.calmac.co.uk

Oban to Coll
2 hrs 45 mins
All Year
Caledonian MacBrayne
08000 66 5000
www.calmac.co.uk

Oban to Colonsay
2 hrs 20 mins
All Year
Caledonian MacBrayne
08000 66 5000
www.calmac.co.uk

Oban to Craignure
45 mins
All Year
Caledonian MacBrayne
08000 66 5000
www.calmac.co.uk

Oban to Lismore
50 mins
All Year
Caledonian MacBrayne
08000 66 5000
www.calmac.co.uk

Oban to Lochboisdale
5 hrs 20 mins
All Year
Caledonian MacBrayne
08000 66 5000
www.calmac.co.uk

Oban to Tiree
3 hrs 30 mins - 4 hrs 15 mins
All Year
Caledonian MacBrayne
08000 66 5000
www.calmac.co.uk

Rosyth to Zeebrugge
18 hrs
All Year
Superfast Ferry Scotland
0870 234 2222
www.superfast.com

Rousay to Wyre
5 mins
All Year
Orkney Ferries
01856 872044
www.orkneyferries.co.uk

Sconser to Raasay
15 mins
All Year
Caledonian MacBrayne
08000 66 5000
www.calmac.co.uk

Scrabster to Seydisfjordur (via Torshavn)
29 hrs 30 mins
Summer Only
Smyril Line
01595 690845
www.smyril-line.com

Scrabster to Stromness
1 hr 30 mins
All Year
North Link Ferries
0845 6000 449
www.northlinkferries.co.uk

Scrabster to Torshavn
12 hrs 30 mins
Summer Only
Smyril Line
01595 690845
www.smyril-line.com

Stranraer to Belfast
1 hr 50 mins - 3 hrs 15 mins
All Year
Stena Line
08705 707070
www.stenaline.co.uk

Tarbert to Lochranza
1 hr 25 mins
Winter Only
Caledonian MacBrayne
08000 66 5000
www.calmac.co.uk

Tarbert to Portavadie
25 mins
All Year
Caledonian MacBrayne
08000 66 5000
www.calmac.co.uk

Tayinloan to Gigha
20 mins
All Year
Caledonian MacBrayne
08000 66 5000
www.calmac.co.uk

Tingwall to Rousay
25 mins
All Year
Orkney Ferries
01856 872044
www.orkneyferries.co.uk

Tobermory to Kilchoan
35 mins
Summer Only
Caledonian MacBrayne
08000 66 5000
www.calmac.co.uk

Toft to Ulsta
20 mins
All Year
Shetland Islands Council
01806 244219
www.shetland.gov.uk/ferries/

Troon to Larne
1 hr 49 mins
Summer Only
P&O Ferries
0870 24 24 777
www.poferries.com

Uig to Lochmaddy
1 hr 45 mins
All Year
Caledonian MacBrayne
08000 66 5000
www.calmac.co.uk

Uig to Tarbert
1 hr 40 mins
All Year
Caledonian MacBrayne
08000 66 5000
www.calmac.co.uk

Ullapool to Stornoway
2 hrs 45 mins
All Year
Caledonian MacBrayne
08000 66 5000
www.calmac.co.uk

Vidlin to Skerries
1 hr 30 mins
All Year
Shetland Islands Council
01806 244219
www.shetland.gov.uk/ferries/

Vidlin to Symbister
40 mins
All Year
Shetland Islands Council
01806 244219
www.shetland.gov.uk/ferries/

Wemyss Bay to Rothesay
35
All Year
Caledonian MacBrayne
08000 66 5000
www.calmac.co.uk

Westray to Papa Westray
40 mins - 1 hr 45 mins
All Year
Orkney Ferries
01856 872044
www.orkneyferries.co.uk

Wyre to Tingwall
25 mins
All Year
Orkney Ferries
01856 872044
www.orkneyferries.co.uk

...irport (ABZ)
/ 0006
.erdeenairport.com

..ra Airport (BRR)
/1871 890283
www.hial.co.uk/barra-airport.html

Benbecula Airport (BEB)
01870 602051
www.hial.co.uk/benbecula-airport.html

Campbeltown Airport (CAL)
01586 553797
www.hial.co.uk/campbeltown-
airport.html

Dundee Airport (DND)
01382 662200
www.dundeecity.gov.uk/airport

Edinburgh Airport (EDI)
0870 040 0007
www.edinburghairport.com

Glasgow Airport (GLA)
0870 040 0008
www.glasgowairport.com

Glasgow Prestwick Airport (PIK)
0871 223 0700
www.gpia.co.uk

Inverness Airport (INV)
01667 464000
www.hial.co.uk/inverness-airport.html

Islay Airport (ILY)
01496 302361
www.hial.co.uk/islay-airport.html

Kirkwall Airport (KOI)
01856 872421
www.hial.co.uk/kirkwall-airport.html

Stornoway Airport (SYY)
01851 707400
www.hial.co.uk/stornowayairport.html

Sumburgh Airport (LSI)
01950 461000
www.hial.co.uk/sumburgh-airport.html

Tiree Airport (TRE)
01879 220456
www.hial.co.uk/tiree-airport.html

Wick Airport (WIC)
01955 602215
www.hial.co.uk/wick-airport.html

Distance chart

KILOMETRES

ABERDEEN	282	342	337	192	246	224	165	793	362	131	184	362	308	252
	AYR	147	93	119	217	58	322	638	235	156	99	79	504	415
		CARLISLE	54	148	316	150	400	491	93	213	176	160	573	482
			DUMFRIES	117	283	119	364	545	141	182	146	107	538	451
				EDINBURGH	211	71	248	598	167	67	57	195	421	335
					FORT WILLIAM	165	105	808	378	164	155	295	282	195
						GLASGOW	270	642	228	92	41	135	444	357
							INVERNESS	850	419	180	231	399	177	91
								LONDON	439	665	668	653	1023	933
									NEWCASTLE	249	223	262	604	502
										PERTH	53	228	354	268
											STIRLING	176	404	318
												STRANRAER	582	492
													THURSO	191
175														ULLAPOOL
213	91													
209	58	33												
119	74	92	73											
153	135	196	176	131										
139	36	93	74	44	102									
103	200	248	226	154	348	168								
493	397	305	339	372	502	399	528							
225	146	58	88	104	235	142	260	273						
81	97	133	113	42	102	57	112	413	155					
115	62	110	91	35	96	25	143	415	139	33				
225	49	99	66	121	183	84	248	406	163	141	109			
191	313	356	334	262	175	276	110	636	376	220	251	362		
157	258	300	280	208	121	222	56	580	312	166	198	306	119	

MILES